Praise for Michael E.

"It's no surprise that Mike's *Th...*
initiating contact, building tru...
quintessential relationship aficionado. He embraces the science of knowing his
customers, products, and business opportunities to successfully negotiate the
sale, all in an atmosphere of trust and respect. *The Science of the Sale* reveals
Mike's tried and true formula for you to be successful in sales."
**—Maureen Borkowski, Chairman & President,
Ameren Transmission Company (Retired), St. Louis, MO**

"For years Mike has been a trusted partner, bringing together people and ideas
to address issues, identify opportunities, drive innovation, and lead change in
the industry. Mike's ability to work across different industries and companies,
with a multitude of different personalities is a testament to Mike as a person
and to the techniques that he utilized. *The Science of the Sale* outlines the
insights and techniques that Mike used and honed over his long and successful
career. *The Science of the Sale* outlines many of those insights and techniques
that we can use to drive success in the ever changing business world."
—Shawn Schukar, Utility Executive, St. Louis, MO

"Mike brings his experience to bear through a series of thoughtful, pragmatic
observations and advice on the science of the sale. His straightforward and
concise style coupled with his wealth of experience provides the reader with a
clear appreciation for what's important: the value of personal connections and
paying it forward."
—Lisa Barton, Utility Executive, Columbus, OH

"Mike Beehler has been a critical thinker in the Electric Utility Industry for
as long as I have known him. Mike has a passion for sharing knowledge and
encourages others to do so as well. He was instrumental in getting utility exec-
utives together to present at industry panels and events."
**—Scott P. Moore, Vice President,
American Electric Power, Columbus, OH**

"*The Science of the Sale* is an incredibly practical and accessible guide to becoming a trusted partner with any customer. Mike Beehler knows what he's talking
about. A colleague for almost 20 years, I was an internal champion of Mike
and his company not just because of the quality of their work, but because of
the trust and relationship that Mike developed."
**—Jeff Guldner, President & CEO,
Arizona Public Service, Phoenix, AZ**

"Mike's book clearly reflects the genuine, authentic and ethically based style he brought to the market. His sales results and long lasting relationships were based on trust and are a true testament to a values based sales approach."

—Steve Berberich, President and CEO,
California Independent System Operator, Folsom, CA

"*The Science of the Sale* is a fantastic book. It is obvious that Mike Beehler has passion behind his pen. Mike has condensed a lifetime of career success winning customers and building relationships into a comprehensive, strategic business plan for all ages. It is easy to recognize and appreciate his pristine care for customers, and process-driven approach in winning deals plus building long-term friendships along the way. As one of his customers for many years, now I know Mike's hidden secrets, and I am thankful for our lifetime friendship."

—Kenny Mercado, Senior Vice President, Integration Lead,
CenterPoint Energy, Houston, TX

"Having worked with Mike for years in a business client relationship, I can attest that Mike truly knows how to build and maintain great customer relationships. Our business relationship was truly built on integrity and trust. Anyone wishing to learn how to become more effective in the science of sales should definitely read Mike's book."

—Richard Bagley, Vice President,
Transmission Engineering & Asset Management (Retired),
Duke Energy, Seminole, FL

"Mike is a gifted salesman with a unique talent to probe changes developing in society. This book shares the recipe that made Mike so successful in supporting this industry. It is a great read!"

—David W. Roop, Director – Electric Transmission
Operations, Dominion Energy Virginia, Richmond, VA

"I always enjoyed working with Mike. He took the time to get to know you—both personally and professionally. Mike adapted his business offerings to meet our business needs. He was interested in advancing the utility industry as a whole. A true sales gentleman."

—Caren Anders, Vice President, Duke Energy (Retired),
VP/GM Energy, JEA, Jacksonville, FL

"Where is Beehler? Not sure, but just look up above the rest of the crowd and you will see his head! I don't even remember when I first met Mike, but what I do remember is his ability to develop and build a sustained relationship that has passed the test of time—well over 20 years with me. It is clear his job was to sell, but it was apparent that he wanted more... he remembered wives and kids' names, hobbies, and significant events...I was not in sales, but I aspired to do the same."

—Dale Oliver, PE Vice President,
EPM&C Entergy Services, Inc, New Orleans, LA

"This is a must read for anyone who touches the corporate sales process. Very easy to read yet comprehensive and informative, including real world practical advice. Mike's key point of business is people, and from that the idea that friends like to work with friends cannot be overemphasized."

—Duane Anstaett, PE, Retired Executive & Officer,
Evergy, Kansas City, MO

"*The Science of the Sale* is an insightful read for anyone in the business of service."
—Werner J. Schweiger, EVP & COO,
Eversource Energy, Boston, MA

"Mike translates his successful sales career into a clear, concise roadmap for others based upon a foundation of trusted relationships. 'Professor' Mike boils down decades of experience into specific lessons within each chapter with techniques that will stand the test of time in the evolving business world. Mike's successful sales techniques are built on trust, lasting relationships and genuine authenticity."

—Ken Bowes, Vice President,
Eversource Energy, Hartford, CT

"As senior transmission executive for a large utility, I typically resisted cold calls from sales people. How did Mike Beehler enter? He gained the trust of the people who reported to me and worked his way through quality, service and trust. He knows I love to talk disrupting technology, and he can speak about it without selling me anything. He knows I love to help mentor those young in their careers, and he demonstrates the same trait. Friends know one another and trust one another. The right person remains friends after there are no sales to be made. I am proud to call Mike Beehler my friend well after *The Science of the Sale*."

—Michael Heyeck, Founder,
The Grid Group LLC, Westerville, OH

"Michael Beehler's book *The Science of the Sale* uncovers a few key under-lying tips needed to effectively craft a business deal. Mike's astute sense for detail captured in this book is directly a result of having spent a long distinguished career working in a highly competitive business selling engi-neering services to the public and private sectors. Mike is a truly gifted speaker, very personable, and a professional engineer who is well known as an industry expert in today's business community. I have had the pleasure to know Mike on a personal and professional level. He is an outstanding person who has deep rooted personal values as it relates to his family and friends. To me, this book is yet another example of Mike extending his many talents and vast professional experience in a way to assist others. I wish him well with this book and in all of his future endeavors yet to come."

—William A. Johnson, General Manager,
Kansas City Board of Public Utilities, Kansas City, KS

"Mike's passion, authenticity, and methods when working with others is clearly shown in *The Science of the Sale*. As a client and a friend, I can heartily recommend that you read it and absorb the science and methods."

—Paul H. Allen, Vice President Operations (Retired), Nashville
Electric Service, Nashville, TN

"Mike truly practices what he preaches. He provides a critical handbook with an important message that extends beyond business and sales: develop friendships, because in the end, people like working with friends."

—Rudy Wynter, President & COO – Wholesale Networks and
US Capital Delivery, National Grid, Waltham, MA

"Mike Beehler and I have been business colleagues for many, many years now, and I am glad to say that I can also call Mike a friend. The traits that most resonated with me in *The Science of the Sale* were authenticity and sin-cerity. This, along with Mike's passion for industry, growth, and innovation are what makes this book a great read!"

—Chris Kelly, COO Electric Business Unit,
National Grid, Waltham, MA

"Mike Beehler is one of the most authentic people I've dealt with in the T&D industry. He is a master of relationships. Over the years, significant business transacted, and I always felt like I was dealing fairly and with a friend. Mike really knows the science of sales."

—Cheri Warren, former SVP, Network Strategy,
National Grid, Waltham, MA

"I have worked with Mike Beehler for more than a decade, and Mike puts into practice every day what he describes in his book. The Science of the Sale is filled with great nuggets of advice on every aspect of the business sales process."
   —Carol Sedewitz, VP Electric Distribution Asset Management, National Grid, Waltham, MA

"This book is an excellent read for anyone in relationship management and sales. Mike Beehler and his team meticulously followed this blueprint for success and always provided outstanding customer service for me and my team in the electric utility industry. He earned my trust and friendship. My wife, Lauriene, and I consider Mike and his wife Dianne friends for life."
   —Walter Spansel, Former Vice President and Transmission Officer, NV Energy, a Berkshire Hathaway Energy Company; Former Director, Transmission, Southern California Edison, Las Vegas, NV

"Michael Beehler has written a must-read for anyone already in sales or about to launch into sales. It gets to the fundamentals of building trust and creating enduring customers...Something he did over and over again in his own career."
   —Marie Jordan, President and CEO, Peak Reliability, Portland, OR

"Much has been written recently about authentic leadership. Anyone who has worked with Mike Beehler has seen authenticity, character, and integrity applied to sales and resulting in high value business relationships that are sustained for many years. In *The Science of the Sale* he has managed to bottle much of his successful approach to sales in a very practical handbook covering the entire sales cycle. His candid and straightforward sales guidance is anchored in a genuine interest in the industry and the people he served"
   —Mike Sullivan, Management Consultant and Senior Vice President (Rretired), Pepco Holdings Incorporated, Washington, DC

"Mike Beehler lives *The Science of the Sale* every day. He exemplifies emotional intelligence, passion for the industry, and lifelong learning. This book provides a deep insight into the value of relationship-based salesmanship. He prepares us all for a rapidly changing business environment."
   —Larry Bekkedahl, Vice President Grid Architecture, Integration & System Operations – PGE, Portland, OR

"Mike offered his authentic and tried-and-true recipes for a successful career as the Iron Chef of Sales. Enlightened by his assertion that 'everyone in business is in sales,' his insights in the industry and steps to work with people based on his exceptional past sales experiences and successes are applicable for all business leaders. His belief of sales based on science provides clarity on the subject matter and is attested with stories and examples, and has led to his personal success. He takes the reader through a no-stone-unturned sales journey, starting from the selection of the right talents and key ingredients, acquiring the right tools, learning from subject matter experts through their books, practical individual preparations for a well-planned process, insightful and watchful steps to ensure building of trust and friendship, and how to close a sale and deliver ultimate customer success. *The Science of the Sale* is much more than a practical guide for the sales professionals; it is a must-read for anyone aiming for business and life success."

—Patrick Lee, President & CEO, PXiSE Energy Solutions, LLC., a subsidiary of Sempra Energy, San Diego, CA

"Mike—or "Beehler" as most of us in the industry referred to him—again puts his generosity and caring into action with guidance for the success of others in this book. Knowing Beehler, his tremendous career sales success is captured through him being exactly the right person for the right job in the right industry and at the right time—but more important than any of that, Mike's always been a trusted friend."

—John Hewa, Chief Operating Officer, Rappahannock Electric Cooperative, Fredericksburg, VA

"Distilling his years as a successful sales professional in the very competitive world of engineering, procurement, and construction, Mike has crafted an accessible and practical guide to the science of sales. Replete with how-tos, checklists and actionable plans, this is an excellent guide for anyone interested developing or honing their sales craft and career!"

—Phil Herrington, Senior Vice President, Southern California Edison, Pomona, CA

"I've known Mike Beehler for a long time—*first as a friend, then as a customer*. And that little statement explains what's so special about Mike and the way he partners with people in business and in life. He instinctively looks for things you and he have in common—whether faith, family, sports or business—and sincerely builds on those linkages to develop trust and friendship that goes beyond business and will endure forever."

—Jim Kelly, Senior Vice President (Retired),
Southern California Edison, Newport, CA

"Mike and I became acquaintances through work – and I truly value his thought leadership in our industry. Mike is the consummate executive leader focused on strategy, development of business and people and building strong customer relationships – he ALWAYS inquired if he and his firm were meeting our expectations and what we could possibly benefit from his firm's experience. Together we safely accomplished a very difficult and expensive First Of A Kind project that was vital to the electric system in Southern California. I feel our strategic partnership was successful because of Mike's professional focus and executive leadership."

—Pete Dietrich, Senior Vice President (Retired),
Southern California Edison, Orange County, CA

"If I had read this book and then you told me who wrote it I would not have been surprised. It is a 'Diary' of our long, enjoyable, and profitable (life and business) relationship. 'Friendship' backed with a crazy passion for the technical side of our business. I'd hand this book to my sales people the day I hired them."

—David Mead, Senior Vice President (Retired),
Southern California Edison, Orange County, CA

"Mike is writing from the heart in this book. He truly believes and practices what is written here. Mike and I go back many, many years to a time when he was evolving and perfecting the relationship methods discussed here in. Mike's advice is tried, true and genuine. The concepts are simple and easy to follow if you are truly dedicated to building strong bonds with customers. Even if you are not in sales, the principles work in all business and personal relationships. Anyone on either the sales or customer side of the business equation would do well to study these relationship building ideals and make them their own. I can honestly say that what started as a customer-client relationship with Mike those oh-so-many years ago has grown into a lifelong friendship. Follow Mike's advice—build the trust and the sales, relationships, and friendship will follow!"

—Chuck Adamson, Principal Manager,
Southern California Edison, Pomona, CA

"Have you been searching for winning principles to succeed in a competitive market? Will the emergence of Artificial Intelligence (AI) impact your career? As Michael states in his book, 'The prize for second place is… nothing.' Michael skillfully shares invaluable and proven guidance whether you are in a sales or non-sales role, to help set yourself apart from the competition. These practical skills and techniques will help you to be successful in today's changing and tempestuous business climate while helping you create strong partnerships and lasting relationships with your customers. As a former customer of his, I can attest that he 'leads by example,' emulating all the tools shared in this book. And after my many years as an executive in domestic and international electric utility businesses, I can only remember a handful of business or sales development representatives that I'm able to call a true partner and friend. Michael is one of them."

—Nestor Martinez, Vice President, Engineering and Technical Services, Transmission and Distribution (Retired), Southern California Edison, Pomona, CA

"Mike Beehler's guidance is spot on! Just like Mike, it's honest, practical, and focuses on the value of personal relationships. I always trusted Mike to know his stuff and to have my personal and company's interest as first priority. You would do well to listen to what he has to say."

—William O. (Billy) Ball, Chief Transmission Officer (Retired), Southern Company, Birmingham, AL

"Beehler is really onto something here. Before reading *The Science of the Sale*—and having spent my entire career as a doer, never a seller—if you had ask me whether sales was an art or a science I would have replied that it was closer to the former. But Mike is right on: most of us won't continue to be doers and his methods to get to a deal are useful for all aspects of life where happiness and health are strongly linked to relationships. The work is very well timed with tips on using all of the wonderful technology we have today to facilitate the development of human relationships rather than replacing them. I have been good friends with Mike for over 20 years and can state with certainty that he truly practices what he preaches and it has served him very well. It's a blessing that he has chosen to share his wisdom."

—Bob Smith, VP Transmission Planning and Development (Retired), TransCanyon LLC, Salt Lake City, UT

"Mike expertly relays how he became 'The Best Salesman on the Planet' in *The Science of the Sale*. Spend an evening or two reading his book and you will embrace the idea that you are made for success in sales and in business."
—Patrick Hogan, Executive Vice President, Utility Technology Solutions, LLC, New York, NY

"Mike Beehler has been a well-recognized sales leader for a major engineering consulting company for many years and this book is a great roadmap to a successful career in sales. It should be required reading for all in the field."
—Chris Root, Chief Operating Officer, Vermont Electric Power Company, Rutland, VT

"Mike has taken his years of experience in selling and distilled it to a simple, easy to follow formula that aligns well with traditional, formalized selling processes. A great bolt on to Strategic Selling, Spin Selling and the like, Mike provides insights from his years of success."
—Mark A. Gabriel, Administrator, Western Area Power Administration, Lakewood, CO

"What a fantastic book! Mike has taken his years of experience and put them into a practical guide on how to succeed in the world of sales. You don't have to be in sales to appreciate the value of this pragmatic business book. I love the action items too. Thanks, Mike, for sharing your wisdom!"
—Gregg Lemler, Retired utility executive & current business consultant, San Francisco Bay Area, CA

"Mike has produced an easy read with valuable content. In this world of high tech, A.I., and 140 character epiphanies, a book with repeated confirmations that high touch and relationships matter should help ground all in the sales space."
—Michael Quinn, Vice President Portfolio Strategy & Risk, Energy Industry, Ft. Worth, TX

"Sage advice from a business veteran. Mike has always been the consummate professional, and yet, challenging and inspirational in his thoughts and actions. *The Science of the Sale* is a straightforward, easy read, with some of the most practical business advice you'll ever need to be successful, regardless of the industry you're in."
—Greg Kiraly, Utility Industry Executive & Advisor, Scottsdale, AZ

The Science of the Sale

Published by MBA, LLC Publishing

Please visit mikebeehler.com

ISBN 13: 978-1-7340399-0-0 (paperback)
ISBN 13: 978-1-7340399-1-7 (ebook)

Book design by Adam Robinson

The SCIENCE of the SALE

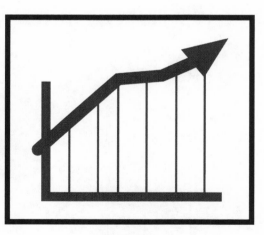

RELATIONSHIPS

SALES

MICHAEL E. BEEHLER

To my loving wife

CONTENTS

"Change before you have to."
—Jack Welch

Sales are based on science. They are not an art. The word science comes from the Latin word *scientia* and means "knowledge." Knowledge, as you will learn, is fundamental to sales. Knowledge about customers, your product or service, the salient issues and opportunities of your industry, and the process of successfully negotiating the price and commercial terms of a contract must be mastered. Art is based on creativity and imagination that appeals to the emotion. Science, in particular social science, deals with individuals and societies through study of communications, economics, history, political science, psychology, and sociology. Engineers, accountants, lawyers, data analysts, computer technicians, and other scientifically-oriented people that excel at the use of knowledge for practical applications should embrace the idea that *they* are made for success in sales.

That's good news because 40-50% of the jobs we do today will disappear in the next 10-15 years due to the science of Artificial Intelligence, according to Dr. Kai-Fu Lee in his fascinating book, *AI Superpowers: China, Silicon Valley and the New World Order.* When I hear predictions like this, I like to ask myself, "What if this is just half right?" What are the ramifications of just 20% of today's jobs disappearing in the next 20 years? Is that your career horizon? AI will not discriminate between blue collar and white collar jobs. Jobs that are hazardous, repetitive, that require little manual dexterity or human interaction are at risk. Jobs that require creative thinking, strategy, or human relationships should provide good opportunities for the future.

Jobs Disappearing in Your Career Horizon

Drivers – Farmers

Printers/Publishers

Cashiers – Travel Agents

Manufacturing Employees

Dispatchers

Waiters and Bartenders

Bank Tellers

Pilots and soldiers

Fast Food – Telemarketers

Tax Accountants – Stockbrokers

Construction Workers – Actors

If your job is on this list, you need to re-invent yourself *right now*. Will your current job be on the next list(s)? What skills do you need to compete with and prevail over the AI robot? Again, the jobs and careers that survive in your career horizon will be those related to creativity and strategy or those that engage with people in close personal and relational ways that computers cannot emulate.

Your best opportunity, and my purpose in writing this book, is for you to learn how to build and maintain close personal and professional relationships that lead to long term business success for all parties engaged. That's called sales. At the end of the day, if you are in business, *you are in sales*.

And, you need passion for sales. If you had to be passionate about sales to save your job, could you do it?

Passion is a fundamental part of The Hedgehog Concept featured in Jim Collin's book *Good to Great*. The hedgehog metaphor is based on a famous philosophical essay, "The Hedgehog and the Fox," by Isaiah Berlin. Collins adopts this metaphor describing how a tiny little hedgehog (representing you) protects itself from the wyly and crafty fox (its natural predator and your competition) by rolling into a tiny, spiny little ball that befuddles the fox and allows the hedgehog to live. Because competition for your job comes at you from all angles, like the hedgehog, you need to rally around your best natural defenses. In the business world, Jim Collins says your best defense and most successful career choice will be the confluence of your deep passion, your natural giftedness, and what best allows you to make money.

The Hedgehog Concept

If you're not passionate about sales, and if a sales-related job just is not your "hedgehog" today, then you need to train and re-invent yourself right now. Artificial Intelligence will not wait for you to catch up. Read this book and do the hard work. There is no prize for second place, and universal basic income for the masses is no way to make your dreams come true.

This book gives you the scientific tools to be successful in sales...nothing artistic about it. I hope that you will love engaging with and serving your customers as they become your career and lifelong friends.

And, ultimately, perhaps you will come to appreciate...the thrill of a sale.

CHAPTER 1

What is Sales?

*"The best way to find out if you can
trust somebody is to trust them."*

—Ernest Hemingway

Sales are built on trust. You establish trust
with a potential buyer by engaging with
them with authenticity, sincerity, and
integrity. These traits are the foundation of good
character, and good character is a key attribute of
leadership.

Merriam Webster's Definition of Authentic

adjective

AU·THEN·TIC | \ AW-THEN-TIK \

1 : worthy of acceptance or belief

2 : not false or imitation : real, actual

3 : true to one's own personality, spirit, or character

We had a Chairman of the Board that risked everything to invest in and grow our company. In his younger years, when he did not own much of anything, he and nine others risked all of their personal assets to purchase a small, Midwestern engineering company. His hard work and business acumen paid off, and over the years he and the other investors grew the company into a national leader in their industry. His sage advice was, *Know Me-Trust Me-Work with Me.*

Get to know your customers personally by being open, candid, and transparent. Your authentic interest in them personally will be evident, and they will appreciate it. As you get acquainted with one another, trust and mutual respect develops into a personal and professional friendship. Ultimately, people enjoy working with friends.

Working with Friends

Know Me

Trust Me

Work with Me

Think about how you like to engage with people. Don't you prefer to work with those that you trust and respect? Friends like to do business with friends. Your honest, sincere and authentic approach to others will pay dividends for your career... if it's real. If you're faking it, people will see right through it. Even for customers that are demographically different from you, you can establish a trust relationship based on their respect for your knowledge of the industry, product or service. I may have grandchildren and my customer just had a newborn, but we can build a relationship on shared industry interests and mutual respect.

Several organizations and professions have guiding principles, codes or cannons to provide direction for working with others. Your company likely has a vision and mission statement and a statement of values that you can follow and emulate as you grow your career.

Vision and Mission

Vision Statement—the long-term reason for your company's existence in 4-5 words.

Sample Vision Statements

Improved Quality of Life

Equal Justice for All

Building a Better World

Peace through Strength

Mission Statement—how your company executes the vision for stakeholders daily

Sample Mission Statement

We will deliver safe, reliable, affordable, and sustainable electricity to our valuable customers. We will be a great place to work and will give back to our communities while providing consistent, market leading performance for our investors.

Rotary is an international service organization that has develop a very popular Four-Way Test as a nonpartisan and nonsectarian ethical guide for Rotarians to use for their personal and professional relationships. The test has been translated into more than 100 languages, and Rotarians recite it at club meetings:

Of the things we think, say or do

1. Is it the TRUTH?

2. Is it FAIR to all concerned?

3. Will it build GOODWILL and BETTER FRIENDSHIPS?

4. Will it be BENEFICIAL to all concerned?

An ethical guide for business. What a great idea. Many other organizations have similar codes and canons of ethics. Engineers, doctors, accountants, businessmen and women, and the military all have ethical standards built on intrinsic values.

Codes & Canons

ASCE Code of Ethics at
HTTPS://WWW.ASCE.ORG/CODE-OF-ETHICS/

Hippocratic Oath at
HTTPS://EN.WIKIPEDIA.ORG/WIKI/HIPPOCRATIC_OATH

US Marine Corps at
HTTPS://MARINEPARENTS.COM/MARINECORPS/MC-OATH.ASP

International Federation of Accountants at
HTTPS://WWW.ETHICSBOARD.ORG/PROJECTS/
REVISED-CODE-ETHICS-COMPLETED

Professionalism Codes of the American Bar
Association at
HTTPS://WWW.AMERICANBAR.ORG/GROUPS/PROFES-
SIONAL_RESPONSIBILITY/RESOURCES/PROFESSIONALISM/
PROFESSIONALISM_CODES/

Decades of experience across the spectrum of industry should leave little doubt in your mind about the importance of honesty and integrity in business. Therefore, as you develop new relationships, build them on a foundation of authentic trust and you will have relationships that last for an entire career and, in some cases, a lifetime.

And, since friends like to do business with friends, you can start to talk about the products and services that you have to sell. It's a natural flow of conversation between two people that have first connected on a personal basis. Sales can be one of many positive results of the new personal relationship you have developed and will maintain over your career. The pure definition of sales is *the extension and acceptance of an offer to engage in business.* Eventually, you can extend an offer for business to your new friend, and when they accept it, you have a customer.

Sales are based on science. The word science comes from the Latin word *scientia* and means "knowledge." Knowledge, like trust, is fundamental to sales. Knowledge about customers, your product or service, the salient issues and opportunities of your industry, and the process of negotiating the price and commercial terms of your contract, all built on a foundation of integrity and trust, is a winning combination every time. So, you will need to be an authentic, real person of integrity and good character, and you will need some basic knowledge about your industry and the products or services your company has to offer. It is at that point you are ready to start growing your career by bringing sales to your organization. What a great way to differentiate yourself from many other talented men and women who want the same promotions and perhaps aspire to the same heights of achievement as you.

The words "marketing" and "business development" are often used interchangeably with sales. To be clear, they are different from, but complimentary to, sales. Marketing uses print, electronic, and social media to "position" a product or service in the mind of the potential buyer. Business development focuses on bringing new products or services to an industry or introducing your company's existing products or services to new regions or industries. The business development process typically takes longer than a sales cycle.

The Same, But Different

Sales—the extension and acceptance of an offer to engage in business

Marketing—using print, electronic, and social media to "position" your company, product, or service

Business Development—introducing products and services to new regions or industries

You will engage with marketers and business developers, but you will have personal relationships that they will likely never have. You can capitalize on these relationships and convert them into business for your organization. You will serve your new customer friends with good value and grow your career at the same time. Then when your boss asks, "what have you done (for me) *lately*?" you will have an answer.

ACTION ITEMS

1. Read *The Speed of Trust* by Stephen M. R. Covey. Open, communicative, collaborative trust amongst co-workers leads to a nimble and entrepreneurial work environment that fosters continuous improvement and, generally, good results. You must read this book.

Chapter 2

Getting the First Meeting

"The way to get started is to quit talking and start doing."
—Walt Disney, Co-Founder, Disney

No matter what business you are in, you need to get in front of customers. If there are no customers, there is no business. When times are good some people may forget and fail to value the people who sell the work. Some are so busy executing the work that they simply don't think about the future. Conversely, in a challenging or start up business environment, people inherently turn to sales. Immediately after September 11, 2001, our CEO assembled the key sales leaders of a then small Architectural/Engineering firm and announced that times have changed...starting now. "Get to the customers now and find what they need, or I will find someone that will." You know that your industry is changing and Artificial Intelligence is rapidly advancing, so now is the time for you to find a way to get in front of customers.

Try these *7 Steps to Finding Your First Customer*:

1. Research the Internet for names of possible customer contacts and make the call

2. Call Supply Chain (or the Purchasing Department) and ask for the contact information for some new part of the customer organization that your company currently does not work for.

3. Reach out to the Supplier Diversity Department and ask for the leader of the customer diversity council and invite them to lunch.

4. Reach out to the Environmental Department and ask for the leader of the sustainability effort or Environmental, Social, and Governance (ESG) filings and ask for an "educational" meeting.

5. Call that friend you met at the local professional society meeting and ask to meet for coffee at their empployee on-site cafeteria.

6. Suggest that your graduate school class meet at a potential customer's workplace so you can become familiar with it and meet other employees as well.

7. Buy the product or service of the customer you seek and then write a letter of appreciation. Get the contact information for the correct person to send such a letter to

and then follow up with a phone call. Ask to meet to discuss the technology of the product or service. Meet at the company lobby or cafeteria or, better yet, the office of the person you are seeing. With that, you're in the door....

You will have a circle of contacts and an influence that no one else has. Develop sincere, authentic relationships with those contacts, develop real friendships, and build your career.

7 Steps to Finding Your First Customer

1. Research the Internet

2. Call Supply Chain

3. Call the Supplier Diversity Dept

4. Reach out to the Environmental Dept

5. Call friend from industry organization

6. Schedule a school meeting on client site

7. Buy the client product or service

Making a call into a client organization can be as simple as getting a person's contact information from the Internet. One young man was convinced that his company needed to be working for a large local manufacturer with offices and plants around the world. He researched the company's website and found the friendly face of the sales contact. Thinking that a sales contact would naturally like to talk, he called the sales contact and asked about opportunities to do business. The sales person was intrigued and connected our ambitious young friend to the plant manager who subsequently invited the caller and his company's team into the plant for a presentation. A simple script for a call could be:

> Hi…my name is Sam Carpenter, and I'm an accountant with KPMG. I plan to be at your office location next week and would love to stop by and introduce myself and KPMG.

Speak slowly and clearly. State your name. State that you are an accountant so they are reminded that KPMG is an accounting/consulting firm. Keep your timing open ended; saying that your plan is to visit sometime in the coming week allows for flexibility with your potential customer. Also, remember that "love" is an emotional word and potential customers love to hear it when you discuss their company, your company, and your objectives.

Script for the Call

Hi…my name is Sam Carpenter, and I'm an accountant with KPMG.

I plan to be at your office location next week and would love to stop by and introduce myself and KPMG.

You can apply the same principles if you are at a plant or customer site. Get to the lunch room, join the local sports league, find a Toastmaster's Club (*I love Toastmasters*—more on this later). Show up early to the client office and stay late. One engineer used to meet every day at 6AM and have coffee with his client contemporaries. He spent the time with the customer, and he learned about their personal lives and design philosophies, system characteristics, personal preferences, and more. His personal touches improved the quality of his already good work and allowed steady repeat business from the customer. Periodically, this client measured our value and when it came time to rank the contract engineers from several competing companies, he was rated #1 out of 21 and kept our team fully employed. The client requested him! He was able to use a field assignment to get to know clients and build relationships with them that no one else could. He created his own sphere of influence. So can you.

First impressions are lasting impressions. It's an old adage, but it's true. When meeting someone for the first time, proper and professional introductions are important. Give the person you are meeting good eye contact (remove your sunglasses if applicable) and a firm handshake. Get their name and the pronunciation right and then repeat their name back to them: "Nice to meet you Karen." The senior person in age or rank would always be introduced first. For example, you would introduce your boss to your spouse first because 1) your boss may be older than you and/or 2) your boss has a superior rank to you in the organization. If your boss came to a customer location and you needed to introduce them to *any* customer, regardless of age or title, you would introduce your customer to your boss since the customer holds the opportunity for business. In this case, you honor the customer by introducing them first. You might say some extra nice things about your boss when introducing them second just for good balance....

Personal Introduction Protocol

Introduce Senior (age or rank) to Junior

State Their Names

"Dr. Smith, please meet Sam Carpenter"

Light Details About Each for Conversation

Eye contact (no sunglasses)

Firm handshake

Get their name right and repeat it

"Nice to meet you, Dr. Smith"

You don't have the opportunity to visit a client site? Go to an industry meeting. Have your boss budget for a trip or better yet write a paper or sit on a panel related to your work. Don't know where to start? Find a mentor that will help you write and submit a paper. I once sat with a senior client executive for the express purpose of brainstorming on program management and how we (together) might apply it to his new $1B megaproject for the first time in the industry. We talked, discussed, and debated the definition and applications of program management. I took prodigious notes. When we were done, he said, "Why don't you whip up your notes into a 20 page whitepaper for me?" I embraced the challenge. I did research on competing methods of project delivery and provided examples of how program management might work in our specific industry. I had the paper peer reviewed both internally and externally with other senior executives in the industry. The final result was a copyrighted industry whitepaper that became the defacto standard and starting point for all discussion about program management at the client organization and, subsequently, with many other customers around the country that were making similar billion dollar scale decisions. And yes, we won the program (and several others in the years to come).

Another way to get engaged with potential customers is to go to a professional society or civic/business group meetings. Start with a local meeting. Join the organization, volunteer for jobs, and seek leadership roles. Soon, you'll have an opportunity to go to state, regional, or even national meetings all while meeting your contemporaries amongst which there will be friends and potential customers.

If you want to maximize your experience at industry meetings, there are some best practices to consider. Always register early for the best "early bird" pricing and stay at the host hotel. You will meet many potential clients and other important contacts in the lobby, elevator, gym, restaurants, etc., and save valuable time by not commuting back and forth to an alternative hotel. Go early to the sessions, events, or meals and stay late. Do not attend an industry event only to be found in your room working on some important deadline. Your company has allowed you to meet and engage with future clients. Resist any temptation to do otherwise. Early in my sales career, I was at an industry conference and walking to the next session or the reception and by chance ran into another guy, and we starting talking. As we engaged, we learned that we had a lot in common given our family and educational backgrounds and our experiences in the industry. We hit it off and stayed in contact over the years. Later, this friend become Chief Operating Officer of his company and was always, and remains, eager to connect with me. This story has repeated over and over for me. Likewise, I would make a point of seeking out younger engineers at technical meetings to recruit to join my growing company. We (I) was making sales, and we needed more talented staff to deliver the promises that I made to my customer friends. I approached this young man and offered my business card and a job interview. He excelled in his interview, joined the company, and is a key leader in one of the regional offices to this day.

Always bring double the number of business cards that you think you'll need. Carry your cards in your breast pocket or purse for easy and convenient access. Have back up cards on your person and additional cards in your briefcase, backpack, or in your room. There is no excuse for not having business cards for potential customers that ask for them.

Schedule customer meetings for coffee, drinks, and meals around the industry event schedule. Always attend all the event meals and receptions. Perhaps, you can arrange to sit together with a potential customer at the event meal. If you don't have plans for dinner, go to vendor hospitality suites and meet people. The vendors want to meet you, and you might be surprised to meet other potential customers at the hosted events. Sometimes, in fact, customers prefer to attend vendor hospitality suites as opposed to a 2-3 hour hosted dinner or event. Finally, you will make many friends amongst the vendor community in your industry, and it pays dividends for your entire career.

Take good notes at the event keynote, speaker, and panel session every day. Don't wait, do it during the presentation(s) or every night before the lights go out while it's fresh in your mind. If there are concurrent sessions, pick the ones that will likely have the most potential customers in attendance. Share the notes with your company when you return. You will prove to your bosses that you attended and got good value from their expense of time and money. Use your notes to remind yourself of action items or promises you made to customers to send links or articles or take some action. Or, send some of your notes to new contacts as a means of follow-up and attempt to get a meeting with them at their site.

Some industry meetings are for-profit ventures and some are part of professional societies staffed by volunteers. In the latter case, meet the organizers, and ask questions about volunteering. Find out when the event organizers start planning for the next session and get involved. It's a great way to meet people and help convince your boss to send you again in the future.

Best Practices for An Industry Meeting

Early bird register…it's cheaper

Stay at the host hotel

Bring double the number of business cards

Go to events early and stay late

Go to vendor hospitality suites

Schedule to meet with customers around the industry events

Take good notes (to share)

Meet the organizers and volunteer

No one has a monopoly on customer relationships. Many people, even professional sales personnel, overstate their "relationship" with a customer. A relationship does not mean you had lunch. You'd be surprised that some claim they "own" a relationship after lunch. A relationship is built over time and is based on personal trust and respect. There are many parts of the customer organization that your professional sales team never gets to. They should embrace your request to find men and women in the customer organization for you to personally reach out to. Look for the new titles in the customer organization. Businesses are always in a mode of continuous improvement (or they should be) with their customers, communities, investors, or other stakeholders. New titles containing words like "innovation, integration, customer, sustainability, smart, or strategic" are great new opportunities for you!

Once you have an invitation to see a potential customer at their location, you need to prepare. If you have started reading *The Speed of Trust* by Covey, you know that communication and collaboration are fundamental to nimble, entrepreneurial businesses. When no one worries about dishonest, back-stabbing "co-workers" lots of good things can happen. Therefore, go to your Customer Relationship Management (CRM) system and find out who is currently working with or pursuing the customer whose location you will visit.

Client Relationship Management (CRM) System

Manages all client data

Is a single source of truth

Is a secure source

Can identify sales opportunities

Records service issues

Manages marketing campaigns

Develops forecasting

Send an email to the names within your own organization that are engaged with the customer and simply notify them that you have been invited to be on site. Think about regional offices that might be engaged with your customer's various regions as well. Then, pick out the senior-most person in the CRM for your new customer and the sales professional assigned the customer and make a courtesy phone call to them. Inform them you are going; don't ask for permission. You have been invited by the customer and you are going. You will, of course, provide details of your visit using the company CRM and other forms of communication as requested.

ACTION ITEMS

1. Find a mentor and write a paper

2. Start attending your favorite local professional society meetings

3. Explore your company CRM

4. Follow the *7 Steps to Finding Your First Customer* and get an invite

5. Communicate

6. Optional Read: *How to Master the Art of Selling* by Tom Hopkins

CHAPTER 3

Preparing for the First Meeting

"By failing to prepare, you are preparing to fail."
—Benjamin Franklin

Now that you have informed the team at work about your invitation to visit a customer, it's time to prepare for the visit. Make sure your electronic calendar has the correct date and time (and time zone) and send the invitation to your customer. The invitation should have an alert set for two days out and a second alert for one hour out. Include your cell phone number and ask for theirs. On the morning of the meeting (or the night before if your meeting is coffee, breakfast, or first thing) you will want to text your customer to remind them of the meeting. A simple text that says, *"Karen, Looking forward to seeing you at your office at 8AM. Enjoy the evening. Thanks, Sam"* will work well. Always remember to use their name and yours. These are early text messages and you should not presume that they have entered you into their contacts…yet. And, people like to hear and see their names…it's more personal. If you do not get a confirmation text that evening, it would be wise to text them about one (1) hour before your meeting in the morning about when they should get their second alert. Receiving no confirmation warrants a quick call.

Get clear directions to the meeting location and put them into your electronic calendar invite for easy access. If you have never been to the location, it's always good practice to drive or walk by the meeting location to make sure you know your way. Sometimes road construction, poor access to parking, walking distances, weather, etc., can impact your arrival time, and you always want to arrive early. Once you arrive at the meeting location or the company lobby, a quick text to your customer not more than five minutes prior to the appointed time is a nice touch. Many corporate lobbies have security and require check-in, a call to the person you are seeing, and a possible security escort. You must allow for the time this will take or you will lose the positive first impression of being punctual and valuable time with the customer. And, early mornings and lunch time are popular times for professional sales people and family and friends to visit customers and employees. Don't get caught in the long lines at the security desk. Always be early.

Research the company you are visiting in your CRM and be up to date on current events and any relevant company news. Your CRM should have the names of people visited by people in your organization, key projects that your company is engaged in, proposals being submitted, and a list of all visits to and touches of the customer. Your professional sales team should be updating the CRM as a matter of best practice. You will also likely be required to do the same and, regardless, you will want to keep a good record of your visit for your future reference. Check the customer website for recent press releases and set your Google Alerts for the company should they appear in the news. You could search for your personal customer contact's name with a search engine or LinkedIn, and some people advocate that. Here's a contrarian view. How would you like it if someone met you for the first or second time and seemed to know a lot about you before you even started talking? To me it's a little aggravating and somewhat awkward. Our goal is to build and maintain personal and professional relationships. A personal conversation about background, family, schools, job duties, etc., is better conveyed for the first time, in person. You and your new customer will freely engage with one another, and who knows what fun, random direction the conversation could take? You want to be remembered as friendly, professional, and unique. You want to be invited back again. When I go to industry meetings, I am always struck by the large numbers of my competitors that are in attendance...sometimes over 1000 other vendors. They all want to see and engage with the same customers that I do. What must I do to be unique and welcomed back time and time again? Starting off with an authentic, personal, and fun meeting is the best way for you to make a positive first impression with your customer. Again, *first impressions are lasting impressions.*

Dress for success at work and especially when you visit a customer. Never underestimate who you might meet when on the customer premise. It is best practice to always dress one level above your customer. If your customer is business casual, then men should sport a tie (Double Windsor knot) with a tie tack and women professional dress or slacks and matching accessories. Business formal requires that men add a suit/sport coat and women a business suit, cardigan sweater, or blazer. If you need to remove the tie or accessories, you can, but you can never upgrade on site. You could discretely remove a tie/accessories if you walked into a room filled with customers that were business casual and they jokingly "asked" you to lighten up and remove an item. Since "many a truth is said in jest," with a smile, and not much production, you would remove the item and tuck it out of sight. Otherwise, keep it on. Be prepared to look sharp with neatly and recently trimmed hair and nails, fresh breath (chew a stick of gum in the car, don't risk forgetting and chewing it on site), and pressed clothes. Have plenty of business cards and a pen in your breast pocket or purse and maybe one or two ad specialties as a leave behind gift for your new customer friend.

The Double Windsor Knot

1. Place tie around your neck with wide end of the tie well below narrow end

2. Cross wide over narrow and hold tight

3. Slip narrow end behind throat and tie

4. Repeat in opposite direction

5. Wide end comes down from top thru new loop

6. Adjust length to top of belt buckle

7. Tie knot should be triangular

8. Pinch sides below knot for indentation

9. Apply tie-tack

Finally, make sure you know your company story. You should have checked on products or services that your company has sold or proposed to your new customer, but be sure to know some your company history, the scope of products and services you provide (even outside your part of the company), your annual sales volume, number of people in your company, and Mission/Vision statement. You never know when you'll need to give an "elevator speech." I have literally been on an elevator and met someone who asked me about my company. Using an economy of words, I had a matter of seconds to convey the "who, what, when where, and why" about my company. One customer that was new to a key decision making role in the organization had no idea who my company was. I provided a simple, professional explanation of my company and the industry educating my customer and making a friend. Be prepared for this...it will happen.

An Elevator Speech

My company (use the name) is the most progressive software designer for the North American banking industry. We were founded in 1981 by two Silicon Valley whiz kids and today we have 250 employees in four major cities, but are headquartered in Santa Clara. We are well known for outstanding customer interfaces and intense cyber security. I have been at my company (use the name again) since I graduated from Stanford in 2010. I love it and work on really cool projects for some of the biggest regional banks in the West.

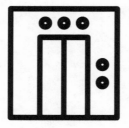

Your early preparation, in general, makes you more confident as your meeting approaches and can provide you with many topics of conversation if and when needed.

ACTION ITEMS

1. Set Google Alerts
2. Read industry periodicals
3. Write and practice (in front of a mirror) your elevator speech
4. Optional Read: *Selling to Big Companies* by Jill Konrath

CHAPTER 4

The Sales Meeting

*"One of the most sincere forms of respect is
actually listening to what another has to say."*
—Bryant H. McGill

The goal of the first sales meeting is to get the
second meeting.

You are well prepared for your first customer
meeting. You are signed in with security and have
your guest pass with your name prominently dis-
played on your right upper chest. By wearing your
nametag as high up on your right shoulder as possible it gives others the best and easiest view of the
nametag and your face. When you extend your right
hand for a handshake, your eye and your arm are
already being drawn to the person's right side and
you can read (and reinforce in your mind) their
name.

Placement of Nametag

Nametag on YOUR right shoulder

Here comes your customer or his/her adminis-trative assistant/secretary to meet/escort you. Your heart is racing and the adrenaline is flowing. Warm greetings are exchanged and you immediately start a personal conversation. This is your responsibil-ity. Walking in silence is awkward and not a good start to an authentic, fun, and engaging meeting. Therefore, be ready. Use their first name (especially for the escort) and talk about something personal, fun, or recent. Using another person's name is important to them and you.

7 Ways to Edify Others

1. Use Their Name

2. Be Gracious and Appreciative

3. Listen First

4. Talk About Them

5. Show Authentic Interest

6. Praise Them or Their Company

7. Sincerely Care

People like to hear their name and appreciate your caring enough to get to know them. If you don't hear your escort's name or get the correct pronunciation of a unique name, lean forward and politely ask them to repeat it. You need to remember their name for the future and repeatedly using it accomplishes that and earns favor. Treating aides, assistants, and secretaries with respect and authentic care and interest will help you in the future. Many times, assistants or secretaries answer the phone or make calendar appointments. Get to know them and treat them well. Talk about the unique weather of the day, how long they have been working at the company, how their week is going, plans for the coming weekend, etc. Allow them to respond and engage in casual, light, and friendly conversation on your way to the meeting destination whether it be a conference room, office, cubicle, or cafeteria. Once at the meeting location, thank the escort, as applicable, by first name, and engage with your customer.

The fundamental rule of conversation with anyone at any meeting or *any* future meeting is engage with them personally before transitioning into a business topic. Always be thinking, Personal-Business-Personal.

When Talking to *Anyone*

Personal

Business

Personal

You are working to build and maintain close personal and professional relationships that lead to long term business success for all parties engaged. Greet your customer with a firm handshake and warm smile. Have a business card ready in your left hand or breast pocket and humbly offer the business card to them with the name/title facing them. In some cultures, the card exchange is a big deal. Basically, do not be flippant about the cordial and respectful manner that a card is given and reciprocally accepted. No need to examine their card. You are not inspecting their title or rank in the organization. Slip their card into your pocket or place it on the table in front of you as you start a personal conversation. Do not sit down until your customer sits down or offers you a chair to sit in. If your customer offers water or coffee, accept it. If it requires a quick trip to the coffee room, go with them and make small talk. If the assistant brings the drinks, thank him/her with direct eye contact and their first name.

Sit straight in the chair with both feet on the floor and both hands above the table. Lean slightly forward to show genuine interest and engagement. Body language is a very important part of communication.

Communication Mythology states that messages are comprised of:

55% body language

38% tone

7% words*

*organized, cogent words still matter

Now that you are settled in, continue with a personal conversation. Quickly scan the meeting area, especially personal cubicles or offices, looking for personal interests of the customer that you can ask about such as family pictures, awards, diplomas, trophies, knick knacks, or project pictures. Customers put the things they care about in their offices. Take their cue. One executive I met had a canned Spam (the scary luncheon meat) collection and another had a larger than life cardboard cutout of him with a king's crown on his head (there was obviously a story there). If you are in a conference room or cafeteria, comment about the posters or pictures on the walls, the views to outside, the contemporary design, etc. Certain industries have a very strong focus on employee and public safety and sometimes have memorials to those that lost their lives in the service of the company. A brief comment to honor the dead and acknowledge the importance of safety is always good practice. Three to four minutes of personal conversation at the start of short (30 minute) meeting is a nice way to start. You will sense when the customer is ready to move into business and then you (or they) can be prepared to transition into a business discussion. Good ways to transition from personal into business include mentioning your appreciation for the meeting in relation to how you both met or set the meeting (See the *7 Steps to Finding*

Your First Customer), current positive news about the customer organization, an upcoming industry event that might interest you both, some relevant and late-breaking industry news of mutual interest, or even some weather event that impacted your customer.

Transitioning from Personal to Business

Appreciation for the meeting

Current, positive news about the customer

An upcoming industry event

Relevant, late-breaking industry news

A weather event that impacted your customer

Your objective during the business portion of your meeting is to learn: Who, What, When, Where, and Why. You will learn this by *listening* to your customer. When you are talking, you are not learning anything.

Your Objective is to Learn:

Who

What

When

Where

Why

Who are the movers and shakers in their company, what are they working on, when will a new product or service be introduced to the market, where will it occur (pilot project or test markets?), and why does your customer think it's happening (what are the drivers)? Listen closely to the answers and ask more questions or, if you have opinions or insights, briefly offer them to start to demonstrate your knowledge and the potential value you could add as a vendor/supplier. Offer your customer any articles, whitepapers, videos, etc., that you are aware of (or could research) and promise to "track it down" and send it to them. Offer to connect your customer or their co-workers with key people in your organization or the industry. Bring your network to them. Successful companies are "continuously improving," usually incrementally and sometimes by "leap-frogging" over their competition.

Depending on where in the organizational structure of a company your customer is currently situated, they may have different perspectives on new initiatives. Junior or less experienced employees of a customer organization can advance careers on new ideas that create new opportunities for them. If you can help them, you add value. Senior and more experienced employees are tasked with bringing continuous improvement to their company and, again, if you can help them, you add value. You bring an outside perspective, you bring news and information, and you bring fresh insights. Thirty-five years later, I still fondly recall the product sales representative that made me successful in my early career by always bringing me whitepapers, research studies, and rich information about the new technology that his product helped launch. I always took his request for a meeting and appreciated his personal and professional interest in me. It was a two-way street; he helped me learn, and I helped internally promote his new technology (that *everyone* still uses today). And, in many industries, it's a small world. The people you engage with early in your career will likely be around for your entire career. People change employers and change jobs within an industry, but in many cases, your paths will cross again. When you think you have the answers to Who, What, When, Where, and Why and have a couple action items that will allow you a follow-up email, call, or meeting, you can start to transition back to a personal conversation and respectfully acknowledge the value of their time. If they look at their watch or the assistant calls or reappears, it's time to go. If you brought an ad specialty, bring it out and place it on the table with direct eye contact, a smile, and a comment about leaving them a little something to remember your company with. Leave something for the assistant and mention them by name. Better yet, hand it to them on the way out.

Perfect first-time ad specialties are inexpensive pens, notepads, lip balm or sunscreen, a travel mug, or a luggage tag. Future meetings might merit ad specialties that match customer's personal interests such as golf balls and accessories, ball caps, leather folders, etc.

Push back your chair and stand up to leave. Shake hands and thank your new customer friend. Recap the action items that you promised to deliver, the personal introductions you will make, and the projected time frame for your deliverables. Promise to reach out the next time you are in the proverbial neighborhood or town or comment that you look forward to seeing them at the next class, the next industry event, or professional meeting. Let them know if they have any questions about what you talked about—personal or professional—to let you know. "Text me...you have my number." Say good-bye and keep personal conversation going with them or your escort all the way out to the exit. Once you reach the privacy of your vehicle, office, hotel room, or home, write down or type out in an email-to-self everything you can remember about the meeting in mostly chronological order. Be sure to have the answers to Who, What, When, Where, and Why as it will help you and your company develop a strategy for future proposals. Write down (and execute) the promised action items and introductions and list the ad specialties you left behind so you don't duplicate them in the future. And, if you did your job, there will be a future. Remember, the goal of the first sales meeting is to *get the second meeting*.

ACTION ITEMS

1. Role play with a friend or spouse. Enter the room, observe the features, start a personal conversation, and transition into business.

2. Optional Read: *Spin Selling* by Neil Rackham

CHAPTER 5

The Sales Meeting Follow-up

*"Diligent follow-up and follow-through will set you
apart from the crowd and communicate excellence."*
—John C. Maxwell

Following up on the first sales meeting is the best way to ensure a second meeting. Lots of people can get a first meeting based on company reputation in the industry, a friendly obligation to help a colleague, a professional obligation to meet with paying customers, or just being nice. But getting the *second* meeting is entirely up to you. You must add value to the relationship either personally or professionally...or both.

Start with handwriting a personal thank you note. In this social media world we live in today, the soft personal touch of a hand-written thank you card is a differentiator. Include your business card and hand write the address on the matching stationery envelope. Use their first name and words that convey authentic delight and appreciation for the visit. Mail it within 48 hours of the meeting if possible.

Thank You Note

Dear Karen,

Thank you so much for taking the time to get acquainted last Tuesday. I really appreciate it and loved hearing about your son's soccer club. Might see you out there sometime with my daughter. Ha. All the best for the coming season. I look forward to possibility of working with you in the future....

Thanks, Sam

Concurrent with the thank you note, you must move at the "speed of trust" and communicate with your company about the meeting you had with a customer. Take your self-emailed notes of the meeting, review and spell check them, and enter them into the CRM. Also, send an email with the notes and a CRM link to the people you contacted before you had the customer meeting, including at a minimum your boss, the senior lead for the customer, and the customer full time sales representative. Include your phone number and availability to talk further as needed.

Separate from the hand-written thank you note, start to work on your promised action items that will prove your value to the customer. Find the papers, presentations, or videos that your company may have. Do your own research if need be. Dig out the contact information on the promised internal or industry contacts. Or, perhaps you made a personal promise. Find that soccer league coach's phone number or link to a great recipe or restaurant that you discussed during your meeting. Put together a nice Personal-Business-Personal email that delivers the promised action items. Do this within a short week of your meeting. Conclude your email with yet another thank you and a promise to stay in touch.

Now that you know the interests of your customer, start to watch for news about those topic(s) of interest. Set your Google Alerts to those topics, scan local newspapers or business journals, and watch the industry news. Look for good reasons to "ping" the customer with very short, but thought-ful, notes on topics that interest them. Become a friendly source of positive information on personal or professional topics for your new customer and add value to your developing relationship. Find out what industry periodicals or organizations are most popular in your peer group and subscribe. You need to be reading about your industry and be a source of information for your customers.

In addition to industry reading, always be pre-pared with an answer to "what are you personally reading?" Personal reading allows you to connect with people on a personal basis. Consider alternat-ing between non-fiction and fiction, balancing work with pleasure. I had a client whose spouse was always asking me what I was reading and enjoyed talking to me about it. Her husband was a great customer, and we developed a close personal and professional relationship that carried over to getting to know her at dinners and industry events. Her husband, and my customer, appreciated that his wife enjoyed our conversations, and we always found a way to get together. She helped to make sure.

Avoid the topics of politics and religion, but have an answer to what you are reading and what cap-tures your attention. Most people know that "lead-ers are readers," and they expect you to be engaged in something of interest. Be ready. "I saw the movie" doesn't count.

Topics to Avoid

Politics

Religion

Bad News—*be positive and happy*

Attempted Dry Humor

Anything Connotative

In anticipation of being successful in sales, join your company or local Toastmaster's Club to practice your speaking and presentation skills. I love Toastmasters! Toastmasters International is a non-profit educational organization that teaches public speaking and leadership skills through a worldwide network of clubs, helping you become more confident speaker, communicator, and leader. Join now and start practicing in a safe and fun environment. Meet people from around your organization that will be resources and friends for you in the years to come.

Think of friendly ways to engage your customer after the first meeting and make them interested in the next meeting. The second meeting is where you might "extend an offer to engage in business."

Stay in Touch

Google Alerts for Company

Adverse Weather

Sports Team Win or Loss

Birthdays/Special Occasions

Favorite Hobby

Some have claimed that it takes at least seven "touches" with a customer for them to remember you and buy. A touch is a sales visit, a mailed thank you note, an action item email follow-up, a quick text on the result of some personal or professional news of interest, their visit to your website to download the paper or video that you sent the link for, etc. Your marketing brochures, print ads, radio or TV ads, billboards, or social media banner ads *supplement* a sales touch, but do not make a sale. Seven times, in today's world of websites, apps, social media, and social selling, is a highly debatable. Regardless of the real number, it's probably much more. If you are not in front of your customer and personally engaged, your competition will be.

Seven Touches

1. First call for meeting

2. Sales visit

3. Mailed thank you note

4. Action item email follow-up

5. Text on personal or professional news

6. Website visit for the link you sent

7. Printed and social media materials

ACTION ITEMS

1. Optional Read: *Perfect Selling* by Linda Richardson

2. Join Toastmasters and earn your CTM

3. Always be reading. Join a book club or go to the library. Start with the Jim Collins books *Good to Great, Great by Choice*, and *How the Mighty Fall*

4. Attend company sponsored educational classes on contract law and new products or services

CHAPTER 6

The Next Meeting: Adding Value...
Every Time

"Stop selling. Start helping."
—Zig Ziglar

After several contacts with the customer, it's time to get invited back. Regular contact with your new customer should garner some reciprocation. They will likely respond to your personal or professional touches with short, quick responses or a thank you. If you have been an authentic and friendly person that followed up on all the promised action items, you have a very good chance of getting the second meeting.

Start the request for a second meeting with a friendly email to your customer (and copy their assistant as applicable), stating that you will be back in the area/office in two to three weeks and would love to swing by and say hello. Hint at some new information on a personal or professional subject of interest and comment that it would be "fun" to re-connect and discuss it. Propose a meeting for lunch, breakfast, coffee, or a drink after work. If you don't hear back within 24 hours, give them a friendly call.

Follow-up Email

Karen, I hope you had a great weekend. Wow your team did really well…congrats. I'm planning to be back in your office in about two weeks and would love to swing by and say hello (again). I've been thinking a lot about the items we discussed last time and have some ideas that I'd like to share with you. Might you be available for lunch on either the 15th or 16th? Breakfast would work as well. Thanks for the consideration. I look forward to seeing you soon. In the meantime, enjoy this beautiful seasonal weather and watch out for the soccer balls…ha…. All the best. Sam

Set and prepare for your second meeting with your customer just as you did the first. Remember, your goal is to build and maintain close personal and professional relationships that lead to long term business success for all parties engaged and your approach should be Personal-Business-Personal. The difference in the second meeting will be 1) you need to add value by bringing a new product sample, a whitepaper, a copy of an industry magazine, or something tangible (not an ad specialty...yet) to give them as you settle into your meeting 2) you will ask them if they might be interested in using your product or service, and 3) you need to find out how you (and your company) can get on the approved vendor or bid list for future opportunities.

A second meeting may be a good opportunity to meet over breakfast/coffee or lunch in the company cafeteria or a nearby favorite restaurant. A simple drink in the cafeteria works as well. It should be a fun and engaging time. If your new customer friend offers to drive, feel free to accept, especially if your vehicle is small, not clean, or is a ride-share.

When dining or having coffee/drink with a customer, always allow the customer to recommend their favorite local spot (and remember it). They probably get invited out often, and if they share a favorite spot with you it should be remembered. As you are seated, face the door, if possible, so you can see others entering the room. It's very likely that their co-workers will frequent the same cafeteria or establishment, and if you face the door, you can see them coming.

Always ask the name of the server and treat them with courteous respect. Use the menu and order something fast and simple. Avoid finger food or messy items like spaghetti or corn on the cob. Sometimes, you might have a buffet option, but resist it if you can. You wanted to spend the limited time that you have with your customer and not standing in line for food. No alcohol at lunch. Most, companies have *a no alcohol policy* for lunch, and everyone should assume that you are all returning to work.

Guide the conversation using Personal-Business-Personal. Have fun. Be sure to respect their time and allow for travel time to and from the location. If they have a 1PM meeting, make sure they are not late because of some long story you shared or a mis-calculation of traffic, etc. Discretely ask the server (by name) for the bill and pay it. Once you have extracted your form of payment, keep your wallet below the table. If your customer cannot accept lunch due to company gift policies, split the bill. Or, if your customer insists on paying, respectfully allow them and thank them. Tip well for good service and thank the server by name. Your customer is watching how you treat other people that you will likely never see again. It's a strong reflection of character. Finally, keep the conversation going at all times during departure and return.

The Lunch Meeting

1. Allow the customer to recommend their favorite lunch spot (and remember it)

2. Face the door if possible

3. Get server's name

4. Use the Menu

5. Avoid finger food

6. No alcohol

7. Guide the conversation

8. Respect their time and allow for travel time

9. Pay the bill

10. If customer can't accept lunch, split the bill

11. If customer insists on paying, allow them and thank them

12. Tip well for good service

13. Keep the conversation going at all times during departure and return

When you depart from your second customer meeting, you'll want them to commit to sending you the contact information of the technical and supply chain personnel that you and your team will need to engage with in the future. Your company may already be under contract for certain products and services, and that contract may or may not include *new* areas of opportunities, such as applications of emerging technologies or current products or services from different parts of the customer's organization. Your product or service might be sold to one part or region of the customer organization, but missing in others. Get the contacts, coordinate with your team as applicable, and start reaching out to expand your opportunities. Keep in close contact with your first customer/friend and make sure they know what you are doing with the names they have provided to you.

Check with your senior customer leader or sales team and learn if they are aware of certain environmental, supplier diversity, or cash flow challenges or goals that the customer has that you could help the customer meet. Communication is important internally and externally.

Initiate the first meeting with the referral contacts and follow the same plan of action from Chapter 4. This time, however, be prepared for more direct questions about your product or services. Be ready for the question, "Why should I hire you?" Your answers should be direct and to the point and demonstrate your knowledge of their particular need or challenge. Your tone should be confident and your body language open and transparent. Look the customer directly in the eye and state your ability to make them successful. Then, tell a story to answer their questions. People remember stories. You will need answers like "we deliver you measurable value and have customers that will confirm it," "our goal is to make you successful with your customers and other stakeholders," and "I promise you that we will deliver great quality and service." Stories will set you apart from the competition. A story will personalize you with your customer. Draw upon your personal experience in the industry and a lesson that you learned about safety, for example, and relate it to your company's safety record. Describe why you like working for your company and some of the attributes that are important to you and that, likewise, would be important to the potential customer. For example, comment on the numbers of young men and women you met from across the company at the recent company picnic and how excited you are to work at a company with so many smart, ambitious young people. "We hire the best and the brightest, they appear to like it. I know I do." Tell real, authentic stories that answer their questions and reveal your personality, attitude, and character in a fun and memorable manner. Once I was in a customer's office after my company had submitted a huge proposal and presented it. They were going to hire six companies for billions of dollars of capital work over several years in a very large region of the

US stretching from Canada to Mexico. There were seven well qualified contenders. A win for us would grow three regional offices and was very important to us. This key decision making customer began by stating that he thought our price was high and then asked me directly, "Why should I hire you?" I answered with a story. I wove personal insights and feelings about my company and the men and women that we hired and their love of the company and the industry. I talked about our safety culture, our local offices, and our mission statement. I waxed on. I did not answer with a conventional response. I told a long and memorable story. Subsequently, we were selected and then, with great teams delivering all that I promised, we became the number one "go to" supplier for this customer.

Tell A Story

Your personal experience in the industry

Why you chose this industry

Your most interesting project

A lesson you learned

Why safety matters to you

Why you like working for your company

The future of the industry; why it excites you

Build Personal Stories Around Sales Attributes

Safety

Cost/Value

Quality of Staff

Location

Schedule

Your Corporate Mission Statement

Diversity

Innovation

If your new customer is ready to engage in the next steps, be prepared to provide them with your company's official contact information for new opportunities. Your company probably already has a point of contact for the customer and you will want to maintain that. You will have been in regular contact with this internal sales person anyway. If not, you can provide your information to this person and receive the vendor correspondence.

Many Purchasing Departments have vendor information forms that must be completed, and you will likely be asked for a Statement of Qualifications (SOQ), product specifications, and references. The pre-qualification process for vendors can be lengthy, and you will need to maintain personal contact with your customer/friend throughout the process. You need to start looking for an "internal champion" within the client organization to help you become an approved vendor and to help you "sell" within the organization. An internal champion can help you navigate the customer hierarchy, understand the corporate culture, and understand approval processes and their related personalities. It will take time to identify and earn the trust and confidence of an internal champion, and they may or may not be your new customer/friend.

The attributes of an internal champion are spelled out in the acrostic CHAMP:

Competitive and wants to win
Honest and provides valuable insights
Attitude that attracts followers
Management credibility and trust
Profit professionally with the success of *your* product/service

After you are qualified to bid or offer proposals to the customer, you can expect to receive a Request for Information (RFI) or a Request for Proposal or Quote (RFP or RFQ). An RFI comes when a customer has a general idea of their project and seeks to further pre-qualify vendors by asking for more general information about a particular, but sometimes not fully defined, need. Often, an RFI response will include a cover letter, customized SOQ, references, a general approach to work, possible teaming arrangements, and some indicative pricing. The cover letter should feature key differentiators of your company from the competition and start to lay the foundation of a proposal, presentation, and, ultimately, a sale. Words matter, so be careful of your word choice and grammar, especially in the cover letter.

Superlatives and Words to Avoid

Perfect

Great

Ensure

Guarantee

Pitch

Maybe

Obviously

Super

Chasing (a project)

Anxious (vs eager)

Problem

Cheap

Fantastic

The RFI process narrows the field of approved vendors that will ultimately receive the RFP/RFQ. The Request for Proposal seeks specifics about scope, schedule, product specifications, commercial terms and conditions, references, personnel, organizational structure, licenses, bonds, insurance, etc. The response to the RFP, called the Proposal, is a much more complex document and can actually become part of the final contract for products/services in many situations. Therefore, preparing a quality proposal is fundamentally important and will require a strong team approach for success.

ACTION ITEMS

1. Optional Read: *Secrets of Closing the Sale* by Zig Ziglar's

2. Write a Paper and submit it for publication in industry periodicals or meetings

3. Attend an industry meeting

4. Prepare an answer for "Why should I hire you?" and practice it out loud in front of a mirror

CHAPTER 7

The Sales Proposal

*"The first step in exceeding your customer's
expectations is to know those expectations."*
—Roy H. Williams

Congratulations, you have received the
RFP/Q and now need to respond with
your best proposal. You worked hard to get
the RFP/Q. Maybe you offered ideas, specifications,
project approaches, or unique perspectives that your
customer/friend was able to incorporate into their
RFP/Q. Helping on the RFP/Q, especially for new
products, new project delivery methods, or emerging technologies, is a great opportunity for both
parties.

You should immediately thank your customer/
friend, your internal champion, and others that
helped along the way with a promise that you intend
to offer a great proposal. In time, your personal and
professional relationship may be so strong, built
on integrity, competence, and trust, that your customer /friend may directly award a sale to you and
your company. However, this comes with years of

excellence and experience (which will be discussed in Chapter 12).

Proposal writing is a process of continuous improvement. You will likely be among 3-5 companies selected to offer a proposal. The prize for second place is…nothing. After notification, the losers will ask your customer/friend's company Purchasing Department for a de-brief on why they lost and how they can improve. Accordingly, their proposal will improve the next time around. Therefore, if you are not continuously improving your Proposals, you will soon lose to the competition. Proposal writing is a team effort. A proposal that responds to an RFP/Q will have several parts, including but not limited to: a cover letter, an executive summary, a project approach or product specification, an approach to work/manufacturing, an organizational chart with resume/CVs, a schedule, pricing, and contractual terms and conditions.

Components of an RFP/Q

Cover letter

Executive Summary

Project Approach or Product Specification

Software, Tools, and Processes Used

Organizational Chart

Resume/CVs

References

Schedule

Pricing

Contractual Terms and Conditions

Bonds and Insurance Disclosures

Diverse Business Commitments

Non-Disclosure Agreements

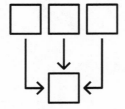

Larger companies have full-time staff dedicated to producing beautiful four-color bound proposals while smaller companies may rely on you, a company principal, and a secretary to produce a simple letter proposal. Appearances aside, an accurate and timely response with strategic content and value is what matters the most. Everything in your Proposal should be strategically written to get you "shortlisted" for a live presentation (of 2-3 companies) and into contract negotiations.

The proposal team should meet very quickly after receiving the RFP/Q to develop a strategic approach, and assign tasks and deadlines to various team members. It is surprising how many companies waste precious strategic and creative time delaying a proposal kick-off meeting and then rush a mediocre proposal out to the customer or decide to "no bid" the RFP due to inadequate time to respond in a quality manner. While you may not be leading the proposal process, *your previous hard sales work*, *your trust relationship* with the customer/friend, and *your knowledge* of who, what, when, where, and why makes you a critical part of the team. Your team's strategy for the Proposal should be built around what you have learned, especially if you found a customer/friend using a new technology, service, or product, or that new customer is in a new geographic region. You have the customer knowledge in this case, and you need to "advocate for the customer" in the proposal strategy development process.

A strategy is a plan developed to achieve a goal. Your strategy will become the differentiator between you and your competitors. Select three strategic reasons why the customer should choose you and buy your product or service. Three is the perfect number for the customer (and you and your team) to remember and repeat in your Proposal and subsequent presentation.

Remembering in Threes

3 Wishes

3 Blind Mice

3 Musketeers

3 Strikes

Stop, Look, and Listen

Stop, Drop, and Roll

When selecting your three strategic differentiators, compare your strengths and weaknesses against the strengths and weaknesses of your competitors. Avoid overlapping strengths, defend your weaknesses, and subtly capitalize on the weaknesses of the competition. Your senior customer leader and the sales lead for the customer should know who the competition will be. If not, you can ask your customer/friend or the internal champion who the competitors "might" be. For new products or services based on emerging technologies, your competition could be non-traditional companies that have served other related industries.

Moreover, strong industries that spend lots of money on re-occurring purchases will attract new market entrants. Domestic and international competition will not miss out on the opportunities for long. I watched several large domestic companies successfully enter my industry segment at the expense of incumbents. I saw international companies win work on critical infrastructure projects at prices no one could believe. We watched non-traditional companies take commercialized military technology to our customers, and today we are mindful of the social media giants gathering data about everything and turning it into information with value. Don't get blind-sided. Do some homework on the competition.

Select Three Strategic Differentiators

Constructed Value

Staff/Team Experience

Latest Technology/Material

Exclusive Patented Product

Production Space Availability

Delivery Location(s)

Advantageous Schedule

Plant and Site Safety

Depth of Resources/Capability

Sustainable Approach (ESG)

Achieves Diversity Goals

Local Presence

Your proposal should follow the RFP/Q to the letter, answering each question with a clear and direct response and always looking for ways to weave the selected strategic differentiators or reasons to buy from you throughout your proposal. Once a customer sent us an RFP and buried deep within the scores of pages was a requirement that Fred Flintstone and Barney Rubble be on the team. We saw it and included a line in our cover letter promising to try to get them. Our humor-loving client wanted to make sure that we read the entire scope document, and, of course, we proved that we did. Another time, the client asked for a California registered professional civil engineer, and we offered a California registered *electrical* engineer. The key decision maker was a civil engineer and our proposal was not considered due to non-compliance.

Therefore, your proposal should offer the exact work or product scope and schedule that the customer is requesting. It might be different than what you discussed with your customer/friend, internal champion, or purchasing department contact, but give them exactly what they ask for. Purchasing Departments like to be able to compare "apples to apples" as much as possible. Sometimes, an RFP/Q will allow the vendor to submit alternate proposals that will, theoretically, deliver more value. If this option exists and you have the time, feel free to offer an alternate along with the original. But, if time is of the essence and a late proposal is "no proposal," it is better to have stellar proposal that addresses each item of the RFP/Q delivered physically and/or electronically on time than a weak or incomplete proposal with options delivered late. Remember, your objective is to get short-listed for a presentation and get into contract negotiations.

ACTION ITEM

1. Optional Read: *Strategic Selling* by Robert Miller and Stephen Heiman
2. Meet your proposal writing staff or explore the tools you would use to do it yourself

CHAPTER 8

The Sales Presentation

"A-B-C. A-Always, B-Be, C-Closing. Always be closing."
—Blake, Glengarry Glen Ross (1992)

Great news...you are short-listed and the Purchasing Department would like to invite your team to the regional head-quarters for a 2 hour presentation. The customer has reached out to you or your designated point of contact and would like to know the date and time that your team can appear in another city to present your proposal to the selection committee. A quick phone call from the sales leader or you notifies the team of the invitation and checks the availability of key staff to attend the out of town meeting. You have the option of selecting your date and time, but its first come first served. You can present first, in the middle, or last.

The advantage of going first is that you can set a very high standard for others to follow. Pick going first if you have market advantage with a unique, patented product and have a very talented project team that matches well with the customer organization. By now, you should have a good idea of what parts of the customer organization will be engaged with the successful bidder and which of them may be on the selection committee. You should form your presentation team to demographically, personally, and technically match the customer project team and/or selection team as much as possible. For example, a customer with a strong preference for local, diverse suppliers should be matched up with a project/product team from your company that has matching diversity and some local/regional proximity. Like the first sales meeting that starts off personal before discussing business, you will want to match the demographics and technical knowledge of your team to specific members of the customer selection team so that they can engage in a personal conversation as the meeting starts to assemble. In addtion, if possible, match similar ages and genders. Other advantages of going first in a competitive presentation process is that the selection committee is fresh and rested and has not been subjected to *boring* PowerPoint presentations. They are generally excited about the new purchase and will be engaged with your presentation. Going first is my personal preference.

I am not a big proponent of going to a presentation in the middle of the short-listed teams. There's a risk of waning interest from the selection committee, schedule changes for some of the selection committee that think they could skip one presentation (yours) and still be part of the selection process, and becoming lost in the shuffle. My preference is to go first or last. Even though the selection committee should ask each presentation team the exact same questions, sometimes they have developed new perspectives that may be reflected in the manner or tone that they ask a question based on the other presentations. They may focus on production capacity or delivery schedules or the resume of your project manager after hearing the strengths, or weaknesses, in the previous presentations. Finally, going last allows your team to respond to any "word on the street" amongst competing vendors and gives you the opportunity to leave the last, best impression with the customer.

Once you have been short-listed for a presentation and you have handpicked your demographically strategic presentation team (that closely matches your proposed organizational chart), you need to plan out the presentation. The presentation should adhere to the format of your proposal and emphasize your three strategic differentiators regularly in strict accordance of the rules and timing allowed by Purchasing. Sometimes, Purchasing states that "no sales" pitches are allowed, they enforce a hard stop at one or two hours, or they require your proposed key leaders to be in attendance. Pay attention to these details of the presentation and fully incorporate them. A PowerPoint or equal presentation is not required, but may times becomes the default method of conveying lots of information quickly, accurately, and in a manner that can be remembered. Regardless, the presentation team should assemble the night before the presentation to practice together their respective roles. The sales lead for the customer should require this meeting and facilitate it. No excuses the next day for stumbling on strategic differentiators, key talking points, or solid answers to tough questions. If a team member won't practice, remove them from the team.

There are best practices for a sales presentation that each presentation team member needs to be aware of. You or your sales leader needs to communicate these best practices to the team. If you need to lead on this, do it. This is your customer that you have developed and here's the chance to impress them. *Winging it* because the senior team thinks they are "just that good" is a recipe for second place. The prize for second place is nothing.

Employ these ten best practices in your presentation:

1. **BE NIMBLE**   Times and locations change, audio-visual equipment fails, people get sick, etc.… and your team needs to be flexible and prepared. Inevitably… something will change. Once we had a major proposal to a new customer, and their new LCD projector failed. We had prepared hard copies and had a back-up presentation using transparencies. We gave the presentation, impressed the client with our preparedness, and won the contract.

2. **TURN OFF YOUR DEVICES**   No cell phones should ring or email notifications chime during a customer presentation. Think it could never happen… think again. Don't let it be your team… it's rude.

3. **ASSIGN TEAM MEMBERS TO THE CUSTOMER SELECTION TEAM**   Each member of your team should have an assigned customer to engage with. Match the demographics and roles within the organization or, better yet, some strong personal interest that you are aware of. For example, a youth soccer referee/coach with a parent with children in youth soccer. We once matched a customer Spring turkey hunter with a hunter from our team… they had a great time.

4. **PERSONAL, BUSINESS, PERSONAL**   Every introduction, encounter, or meeting starts with something personal. Do NOT talk business until you have engaged with someone personally. Then, conduct the business of the meeting, presentation, or round table discussion and conclude with something personal. Everyone on your team has an assignment after the presentation. It can be as simple as making comments on the weather, the local sports team, or plans for the weekend. Mentioning the common interest in soccer or hunting would be most effective on the way out the door and all the way to the exit.

5. **A SAFETY MOMENT**   Depending on your industry, all meetings will start with a safety lesson, locations of exits, and assignments for calling Security/911, CPR, etc. Your team should be prepared to comment on your safety culture or generally comment on your appreciation for safety with a personal, but very positive, story.

6. **SALES REP LEADS WITH INTRODUCTIONS**   The person that leads the sales presentation should introduce each member of the proposal team to the customer. They can say more nice things about each team member than someone will tend to say about themselves. Humility is good for the individual, but some-times the humble approach leaves out key details and fun personal notes that the sales lead can share. The sales lead should think about this in advance and be prepared with proper name pro-nunciation, titles (or roles in the proposal), and some good relevant and fun facts about each team member. Once we attended a very large customer presentation where we were seated classroom style. The customer invited us to go around the room for personal introductions. I was the sales lead for the team and knew several of the clients in the room. When it came my turn to introduce myself, I started by telling a story about one of my client friends. He had moved north to this new company and was excited because he could "get in a few more weeks of ice fishing." I told

the "ice fishing" story and for the balance of the introductions, people laughed and had fun with the subject. When my friend had his turn, the fun continued. A simple story helped us start off a long presentation on a great personal note.

7. **RAPT ATTENTION**   When your team is presenting, each of your team members must pay attention. No open laptops, texting, eating, or doodling. At one large presentation that I attended, I watched and smelled as one of our team members unpeeled a banana and discretely ate it while our team lead was presenting at the front of the room. The smell of banana wafted through the room. You want to model for the customer how to listen. There is nothing more interesting going on anywhere that could distract you (or them). Pay attention to when they take notes and watch their body language. These are good indications of topics that you could reinforce or revisit as needed.

8. **WATCH THE CLOCK**   When a customer sets a time limit for your presentation, it's usually a hard stop. Purchasing departments, in particular, will enforce this. Always make sure you have adequate time for EACH of your presenting team members to present their part of the proposal and address possible questions. Questions may be reserved for the end, but inevitably some will be asked and you must account for it. Each of your

team members should have practiced their presentation out loud during your practice session or even alone, in front of the mirror, the night before. But if someone gets verbose, the sales leader must politely let them know. It can be as simple as stating to your team member by name. "Mike, those are important points, but you have about two minutes left before we need to hear from Mary."

9. **KNOW WHEN TO STOP**   As the opportunity to close a successful presentation approaches, do not allow team members to re-open technical or commercial topics. Advise them in advance. Once a customer is favorable to your proposal, you do not need to do more. Your goal is to get to the negotiating table, and if you are heading towards negotiations there is no reason to allow a silly mistake or strong ego to potentially undo all that was accomplished by the team's presentation. Stop presenting and start closing.

10. **LEAVE TIME FOR CLOSE**   Allow at least 10-15 minutes at the end of your presentation and the Q&A period to wrap up your most important points, the key value proposition, the three differentiators, your strong desire to work together, or your respect and admiration of their organization. The customer will need time to reciprocate and thank you for your time and travel. This is a great time to get a sense of how

you were received. A quick review by the sales lead of any action items would be appropriate and, then, shift into personal mode. Allow the customer to adjourn the meeting and start to stand up and then you should follow the customer's lead. All conversation is now personal.

Best Practices for the Presentation Team

Be Nimble

Turn Off Your Devices

Assign Team Members to Customer
Selection Team

Use the Personal-Business-Personal model

Take A Safety Moment

Sales Rep Leads with Introductions

Keep Rapt Attention

Watch the Clock

Know When to Stop

Leave Time for Close

The PowerPoint or equivalent presentation should contain slides with NO MORE than three topics, stated in 3-5 words. A recent, relevant, and regional picture that matches the limited text should be included. For example, when presenting in a coastal environment like south Florida, pictures of sunshine, palm trees, and Florida landmarks make sense. No accidental mountains or landmarks/infrastructure from other locales. The picture should be a topic of conversation and reinforce a point that needs to be made in the proposal you are presenting. Remember, a picture really does say 1000 words.

PowerPoint Presentation Basics

Recent, Relevant, and Regional

One Picture

Three Bullets of 4-5 words MAX

- **A New Paradigm of Thinking**

- **Your Future**

- **Start Now**

PowerPoint or equal presentations are not always needed. Sometimes a round table discussion of the proposal and an amiable question and answer session can work well. The round table discussion should have an agenda and needs a strong sales or team leader to control and maintain the strategic focus of the discussion and follow the agenda. Key points of the proposal and the proposal differentiators should be assigned to various members of the team to specifically discuss during the round table. A practice session is still needed before the customer meeting. Communications is a combination of words, tone, and body language. Make sure that you and your team have open and confident body language using direct eye contact and smiles. The tone of voice should be friendly, positive, and enthusiastic. Remember, your customer may be deciding who they want to work with for the next few months or years and negative, monotone, sarcastic, and generally unfriendly tone of voice will not help your team. Finally, word choice is important. The words your team uses should be positive and team oriented. There are no problems, only challenges. You are never anxious to work for a client, only eager. The word "team" is not spelled with an "I," therefore always, always talk about us or we…. Believe it or not, this takes practice. You are still selling at this point, and your objective is to get the negotiating table.

Negative vs Positive Word Choice

Problems vs Challenges

Anxious vs Eager

I vs We

Cost vs Value

All vs Most

Shall vs Will

Market vs Industry

Dangerous vs Hazardous

Hire vs Consider

Best vs Reasonable

Always consider extra touches that will etch your team into the minds of the selection committee.

Ice breakers…something to get a conversation started. One presentation that I attended, the PM brought the real Ice Breaker candy to lay out on the table to figuratively make the point about getting acquainted (the personal introduction part).

Placemats with the proposed organizational chart, short personnel bios, or some pictures from your proposal along with your three differentiators can be a nice touch as well.

Posters of fictitious local newspaper headlines showing on time completion, your customer comments about their satisfaction, or a quote from an antagonist stating how satisfied they are after all. Mount the posters on foam board and set them on the whiteboard in the room or ask for a flip chart with an easel and set the poster on the easel as the customer enters the room. Leave the posters for the customer. Maybe your competition will see it and comment on it. That's more name recognition for your team.

Use hand held signs with catchy phrases to keep the customer interviewers engaged with you. "Really?" "You're Hired!" "That's Not What Your Competition Said." or "Tell Me More!" are fun, light hearted ways to make you and your team memorable to those that may not know you.

Videos are possible but should be used sparingly unless they present a key team member that cannot attend, provide a unique CEO promise, feature customer reference statements, or showcase something extraordinary like a 3D flyover of a completed project or product application. I favor a strong focus on personnel that are live and present in the room. It's more personal and direct. You could have emailed them a video. They need to meet your team and gain confidence in them, personally.

3D models of your product or completed project that customers can look at, touch, and talk about should be spread amongst the customers around the table. 3D printed models also demonstrate your technical acumen and can lead to great side conversations about your ability to use augmented and virtual reality.

Logoed pens and notepads for customers to take notes and then to keep are a simple extra touch and should always be used.

Extra touches and going the extra mile in a presentation is important. Have no regrets…your company is counting on you to get to final negotiations.

ACTION ITEMS

1. Optional Read: *The Greatest Salesman in the World* by Og Mandino's

2. Develop a list of tough questions that you could be asked at a sales presentation and practice your answers

3. Write your own fictitious newspaper article for completed project to be used as a presentation prop

CHAPTER 9

Contracts & Negotiations

"Get closer than ever to your customers. So close that you tell them what they need well before they realize it themselves."

—Steve Jobs

Your proposal got shortlisted, you presented your product or service to the customer, and they like it. Now, you are invited to the table to negotiate your contract. A contract is simply a written offer and acceptance to provide a product or service for a mutually agreed upon consideration with obligations that are enforceable.

Entire books are written about contract negotiations, but it can be broken down into some simple steps. First, understand that everyone's time is valuable. You are at the negotiating table because your customer really does want to work with you. Occasionally, the customer will negotiate with two or more companies concurrently, but some consider that offensive and slightly unethical. Your friends in the organization should be able to discretely advise you if their supply chain is playing you against your competitor. However, be aware that many times there are clear instructions during a procurement process about interaction with customer personnel. Be sure not to violate this policy since it could be used to disqualify your company from further consideration and negotiations. Otherwise, be excited and be prepared. You will not sign this contract because you "got lucky." Hard work and preparation define "luck." Study your proposal and your differentiators, re-read all your sales notes about areas of customer interest and focus, check on current events about the company, and intently read the contract terms and conditions. Current events are important in case some news of a labor issue, safety incident, product failure, etc., impacts their negotiating perspective. At a minimum, you are still in "full sales mode" and need to be aware of your potential customer's issues or challenges. Be very close to your customer!

You have read and studied your proposed contract. Now, you need to determine and understand the parts of the contract that you must have and what parts you can truly negotiate on if need be. Seek counsel from your in-house attorneys, principals, or seasoned negotiating veterans on what to watch for. Negotiating a contract will likely involve going through a contract page by page in a "page turn" meeting. Each item of the contract will be reviewed, perhaps read out loud, and discussed paragraph by paragraph and page by page. It's the customer's simple intent that you and your team understand their terms and conditions of the contract. The process can be long and, sometimes, arduous. Take your time. Explain your position to your customer. Make simple points, in layman's terms, as to why they might want to consider your perspective. Take a break periodically to keep a clear head and engage in friendly, personal conversation with your customer's negotiation team. Perhaps they will share something in a casual and personal conversation that will give you insights to their position. As needed, strategically ask for a break for restrooms or even a smoke (know your client) and use the time for your team to privately confer about an issue(s) that concerns you. Be aware of how voices can carry in enclosed rooms and look for a very private area away from people and possible eavesdroppers

Ten Simple Steps for Negotiations

Check current events

Study the contract

Check with counsel

Do the Page Turn

Understand the Big 5

Explain your position

Take breaks

Don't Rush

Give something back at the end

Be able to walk away

Decide as a team what minor concessions to the contract you are willing to make or accept to initiate positive dialogue and momentum in negotiations. Be free to share minor concessions with your customer and make sure your customer understands that a concession costs you money but can offer them certain benefits or advantages. Quantify the benefits in terms of cost, schedule, quality, safety improvements, etc., if you can. Target these minor concessions to impact some of the customer's most important uses of the product or service you propose or, to relate specifically to an item of interest by one of the customer's negotiators or key decision makers. You are building positive momentum and goodwill early in the negotiation process; you are making progress. Make clear that everything that you give the customer has value and you will expect a reciprocal response. Each concession is contingent upon a similar act of good faith by the customer. If there is no interest in a concession with an acceptable reciprocal response, take the concession off the table and move on. Look for a better time in the negotiations to revisit the opportunity.

There will be certain parts of the contract that are non-negotiable for your company. Every company's risk tolerance is different. Customers will shift as much risk to your company as you are willing to naively take. They may tell you that your competitors are willing to accept their terms, and that may be true. In some cases, you can state that those competing companies that accept unmitigated risks are not actual competitors in any real sense and that your potential customer should be concerned. Some of your so-called competitors may be smaller or newer companies that have no real assets and, accordingly, can take on the liabilities of risk with very little downside.

That's NOT My Competitor

They don't have our *scale and depth of resources*

They don't have our *top tier safety record*

They don't have our *experience* on this kind of deliverable

They don't have a *local office*

They don't meet your *diversity goals*

They don't meet your *sustainability goals*

They don't have *industry thought leaders*

They don't have an *R&D lab*

They don't have *100 years of history*

They don't have the *good business sense* to revise this contract

The risk on any product or service is inherent to that product or service. But who owns the risk is the real question. Emerging technologies, cyber security responsibilities, labor shortages, and other factors add new and complex risks to the delivery of products and services. Money follows risk. Wise negotiation that fairly assigns project/product risk and associated compensation for that risk shows to your customer your business acumen. They should, ultimately, respect you for it and appreciate your competence.

Following the resolution and agreement on minor items in your contract, there are five major concerns found in most contracts for products and services that must be addressed.

The big five concerns are:

1. **CONSEQUENTIAL DAMAGES** typically are the result of your unique and predictable actions that cause damage to the owner or their customers. You want to limit this.

2. **LIMITS OF LIABILITY INCLUDING CYBER LIABILITY** caps or limits the amount your insurance company must pay a claimant per occurrence and in aggregate. You want to limit this.

3. **WAIVER OF SUBROGATION** is when your insured customer waives the right of their insurance carrier to sue you for losses from a negligent

third party like a part supplier or subcontractor. You want a waiver.

4. **INDEMNIFICATION** contractually compensates for the loss incurred by those indemnified or held harmless (your customer) from the actions of the indemnitor (you) or another party (subs or suppliers). You want mutual or "cross" indemnity.

5. **PRODUCT LIABILITY** holds those who manufacture or supply products to the public responsible for the injuries or damages caused by said products. Laws vary from state to state in the US. You want to limit this.

Understanding these five concerns and the reasoning behind them is important. Many times, a concept will be repeated in subsequent paragraphs of a contract, and it's important to be aware of these redundancies when making edits or modifications to the contract. Use word search software to look for key words such as damages, liability, subrogation, and indemnify. In addition, look for simple missing words like "not," the difference between the supplier saying they *shall or shall not* perform said task or deliverable or *shall or shall not* accept liability. Mark these redundant, textual, or other concerns in the margins of your contract and make sure your team is mutually aware of them as you review the contract page by page in the "page turn" meeting. A respectful discussion of the big five concerns will be fundamental to your successful negotiation of the contract. You and your team's ability to clearly and concisely describe the big five concepts and articulate your perspective cannot be understated.

One of the last rules of negotiation is having the ability to say "no thank you" and walk away. It rarely happens, but there is no reason to sign an unfair contract that has terms and conditions that your team cannot successfully and profitably meet. However, at this point of the sales process, most people want to engage and get the products or services delivered. Assuming that all goes well, look for a small bonus item that you can give your new customer that benefits their company and leaves everyone feeling good about the negotiation and final contract. Examples of no or low cost give backs at the conclusion of negotiations are: an added follow-up service, an accelerated timeline for an important line item, a first payment schedule adjustment, hosting a kick-off dinner or team-building event, etc.

Small items that offer your customer an added *end of negotiation* bonus shows your gratitude and long term commitment to them. Showing that gratitude and commitment starts with the signing of the contract and should continue for the life of the product or project, and, truthfully, for your career.

ACTION ITEMS

1. Optional Read: *The Little Red Book of Selling* by Jeff Gitomer. Note: Gitomer's other classic work is *The Sales Bible*

2. Read the contract associated with your customer. If no contract is currently in place, read one for a similar customer. Ask questions

3. Attend legal training classes

4. Have coffee with your corporate attorney... get to know them

CHAPTER 10

Product Delivery or Project Kick-off

*"There is only one boss. The customer. And he can fire
everybody in the company from the chairman on down,
simply by spending his money somewhere else."*
—Sam Walton

The contract is signed. Congratulations,
you now have the opportunity to deliver
on all the promises that *you* made to your
new friends. The challenge will be that many other
people from your company and team will be part
of the product or project delivery. You will need to
maintain close contact with your friends and the
customer organization to make sure that everything
runs smoothly and in accordance with the contract
that you just signed. A great way to start a project
and to make that smooth transition of your project
team onto the customer team is with a celebration
dinner to "kick-off" the project.

The contract will identify the key point of contact for both organizations. If you are not that person for your company, go to the person that is and
suggest a project kick-off dinner the night of the

project kick-off meeting. If the project is small and you are personally involved in the delivery of the product or service, then perhaps just a small lunch with the team. But, bigger projects with people just newly introduced to one another through a proposal or negotiation process need an opportunity for people to connect on a more personal basis. Some companies advocate team building exercises like cooking contests or sailing a boat together. Team building is important, but you can probably accomplish much of what your need with a fun and casual dinner at a moderately priced restaurant. Check with your customer and the supply chain about their entertainment policies and allow them to host the event as needed. Consider inviting spouses or guests of key team members if your customer is amenable.

The celebration dinner is on, and you are in charge. The following are some best practices for hosting a business dinner.

Make the reservation for dinner well in advance. Book a private room at a single long table for parties over six, if possible. Always arrive at the venue 15-30 minutes prior to the dinner reservation. Wait in the bar for your guests to arrive.

Greet your guests as they arrive by their first name. Use nametags for groups over 20 people. Wear your nametag on your upper right chest for good visibility when shaking hands. When shaking hands with your right hand, you naturally lean forward, making your nametag readily visible to your guest. As the host, you will need to introduce your team and the customer and their guests to others. Courteous personal and professional introductions call for you to always introduce the senior person (in age or rank) to the junior person. For example, "Dr. Carpenter, I'd like to introduce you to Caren Smith, our new project manager. Caren, this is Dr. Carpenter, the lead researcher on the new technology that we are deploying on this project."

When the entire party has arrived, but no later than ten minutes after your official reservation, let the host/hostess at the restaurant know that you are ready to be seated. You might text any late arrivals and let them know to come to your table or private room. Allow your guests to sit where they like, keeping in mind that your customers and spouse/guests will likely want to sit together. It is an honor that a spouse/guest attends this "business" dinner so make sure that they have a delightful time and want to join you again in the future. If the spouse/guest does not want to attend the next dinner opportunity, the likelihood of your customer attending drops significantly. As everyone settles into their seats, place your napkin on your lap and keep conversation light and free-flowing. Take direction from the server staff as they approach the table to welcome the group.

Be prepared to respond to a request from your server for wine. Alcohol at a customer event or dinner should be in moderation if served at all. Never drink alcohol at lunch. If your customer drinks alcohol at dinner, you may. If your customer does not drink, you do not drink. If your customer is a wine connoisseur, offer them honor of selecting the wine. You will have to trust their moderate tastes, if you are hosting.

Select a dinner entree that is moderately priced and easy to eat. No king crab legs or spaghetti. Choose a soup/salad and entree that is an example of reasonable price points for your team and your customer to follow. If you are the host, you set a helpful example and demonstrate your sensitivity to price (just like on their project). If you are being hosted, again, you demonstrate price sensitivity and respect their generosity of hosting the dinner. Hosted dinners can easily cost $100/person without alcohol, so be price sensitive. Everyone will appreciate it.

Once everyone has ordered their dinner, you might offer a toast. This is a very common practice and gives you the chance to "kick-off" the project in style. A great toast has several components. Tap your glass with your knife and get everyone's attention. For larger groups, stand up and smile and offer the toast. You need to be able to give all the people around the table or the room good eye contact. Start by saying that you are grateful for their trust and confidence. State that you respect and admire each one of them and call some out by name if you know them. Let them all know that your team is excited to be working with them *on this project* and give accolades *for the new team* gathered around the table. Raise your glass, smile, and say "here's to the team!" Sometimes, your customer guest will reciprocate.

Template for a Great Toast

G-grateful for their trust and confidence

R-respect for the *clients by name*

E-excited to be working *on this project*

A-accolades for *key leaders*

T-*team*

As the food arrives, remember that manners count. Some people know and appreciate good manners and some people don't know or care. It's better to assume that everyone knows and cares, because you don't know otherwise. Your drink is on the right over your knife and spoon and your bread plate is on the left over your fork. Always start with the utensil on the outside first and work inward from there. Entire books are written about etiquette and manners. See Emily Post's book on etiquette at HTTPS://EMILYPOST.COM/BOOK/EMILY-POSTS-ETIQUETTE or look up Beaumont Etiquette, a contemporary finishing school ensconced within Midtown's Plaza Hotel. The bottom line is use good manners. Never ask or joke about table placement or manners in general, and if your customer uses the wrong plate or utensil, just go with the flow.

Table Setting

Always start with the utensil on the
outside first and work inward from there

Once everyone has received their soup or salad, it may be time for an optional invocation. Most customer dinners will not need an invocation. However, in some cases, for very large dinners at special customer or industry events, an invocation may be appropriate. You should be prepared. A simple, non-secular prayer that respects the many different faiths in the room can follow a template of God, country, company, family, and food (and the hands that serve it). Ask your attendees to "join me in prayer." Thank God for a beautiful day and our free country. Ask God to protect the men and women that preserve those freedoms. Thank Him for the companies that we work for and the products and services that we deliver for people. Thank God for our families and ask Him to keep them safe while we are away. Thank Him for the food and the hands that prepared and served it. A simple Amen quickly followed by a comment from the prayer giver about the great location, menu, new project, etc., will break any awkward post-prayer pause.

Template for an Invocation

Thanks to:

God

Country

Company

Family

The Food and That Hands That Serve It

Amen

Always be mindful of your customer's precious time with their spouses and families, and end the dinner when everyone has finished the last of their dessert and optional coffee or after-dinner drink. Thank everyone for attending and bid them safe travels home. As people rise and prepare to leave, personally thank each person and their spouse/guest for attending. Keep everything personal. This is the time to reinforce the personal relationships on which good business is built. It is not the time for any business conversation.

ACTION ITEMS

1. Optional Read: *Mastering the Complex Sale* by Jeff Thull
2. Practice an invocation
3. Practice a great toast

CHAPTER 11

Tracking Progress and Reporting

*"The key is to set realistic customer expectations, and
then not to just meet them, but to exceed them—
preferably in unexpected and helpful ways."*
—Richard Branson

The project or product delivery process has
started and your team is fully engaged
with the customer. The kick-off dinner or
celebration went well and your project manager is
reporting on a regular basis to you and the project
team about the results of their efforts to date. Now,
it's time to trust, but verify.

Project managers tend to say positive things about
their team and their efforts. What's really important
for your company is what the customer thinks. You
went to this new customer or part of the customer
organization first. You now know and have a growing relationship with one or more people within
the customer organization. You made the upfront
promises. Therefore, you need to go back and make
sure that everything is running smoothly. If, in fact,
everything is going as promised, start looking for

new opportunities to expand your company's work and opportunity.

Time your first visit back to the customer one to two weeks before the first project milestone, which may be a 30% design review, a review of fabrication drawing/specifications, or a review of the production schedule. However, don't wait longer than three months after the kick-off meeting that you attended. Call or email your customer and let them know that you will be back in town in a few weeks for the express purpose to follow up and make sure that your company is performing as promised. Some companies use electronic surveys to measure and quantify project performance and customer satisfaction, but the personal touch of a trusted friend is always the best. You have become that trusted friend.

You will be the advocate for this new customer in your organization. You will meet with the customer and eventually ask the tough questions about your company's performance to date on quality, schedule, communication, team chemistry, the first invoice or two, customer safety practices, and more. Many times, you will get an answer that your customer hasn't heard anything "bad' so everything must be running well. The *no news is good news* adage. Make sure you are asking more than one person these questions and watch their reactions. Lack of good eye contact, negative body language, or hesitation in their oral responses may be a sign that something is amiss. Spend more time with them if you can.

Be sure to go to the Purchasing Department or supply chain representatives that you have met and make sure they know that you are following up. You can advise them of who you are visiting with and update them on your progress to date. They will appreciate it, and this meeting will afford you an excellent opportunity to make sure that your company is an approved vendor for any other needs coming up in the future. Be deliberate about asking. If your company is not approved for something you offer, ask what your company needs to do to be considered. You might be very surprised that your company is viewed as a provider of a very narrow scope of products and services. Expanding that scope is your opportunity to expand your company's business *and your career.*

Some organizations use customer satisfaction surveys for monitoring performance. If a customer has responded to an electronic survey, be sure to thank them for their time and comments. Special positive or negative comments in an electronic survey need to be addressed immediately upon receipt by the senior most person on your project. You should be aware of any such activity prior to going back to the customer location and meeting with your friends. This information would be recorded, stored, and managed in the Client Relationship Management (CRM) database. Several large software companies sell these databases, which allow users to collect customer data and turn it into information and, ultimately, sales related action. All of the information that you and the other members of the project team collect should go into the CRM. If done well, you will then find a chronology of events related to your project and to the customer in general as well as collected personal information such as spouse's name, birthday, hobbies, etc. If you find holes in your data about a customer, you can always check their LinkedIn or other social media sites for the information that they allow others to see. If you do not have access to the CRM, a simple word document that records notes of your trips or conversations with customers will suffice. Develop a spreadsheet of contact information data and more that you can sort and merge as needed. You will be amazed at the long term value that these notes and data points provide as the depth and number of your business relationships grows.

Data for the CRM

Nick Name

Spouse Name if any

Children if any

Birthday

Alma Mater and Degree(s)

Employment History

Hobbies

Pets

Favorite Sports and Teams

Boss's Name

You now have a friend or friends in the customer organization. They know you, trust you, and want to work with you. But, you will likely start to meet others as well. They won't know or trust you yet, and they may not even be familiar with your company. You might find that you have just replaced their favorite product or service provider. Perhaps, they advocated for the other company during the selection process and lost out. Maybe they are new to the organization or position and need to establish themselves as proactive, value adders. You need to be ready for some tough questions. Be prepared with solid answers to tough questions like: "Who is your boss and why don't I ever see them?" "What have you done for me lately?" or "When will I get the results your team promised?"

Tough Questions with Good Answers

Why don't we ever see your boss?
My boss trusts me to do a good job, but I'd be happy
to have him/her come with me next time.

What have you done for me lately?
In fact, we have some new ideas that we'd like to
share with your company.

When will I get the results you promised?
Where are we missing the mark? And, I will report it
to my team and bosses.

Where did you get your project team from?
This was the team that we proposed. Most of them
come from great local area universities.

Where is the diverse staff you promised?
Diversity is a promised priority. Let me find out
when that part of our team will be engaged.

Why is your price so high?
Our price reflects the total value we deliver and was
part of our contract negotiations at the time.

Anticipating tough questions and rehearsing short, solid answers will help build your personal credibility and, with satisfactory answers, allow you to shift to other topics like what new challenges the customer might foresee in the near future or whether there will be more need for your product or service.

The friendships that you develop in the customer organization take time to mature. Relationships, like love, can be a function of time and are meta-phorically spelled T-I-M-E. The men and women in the customer organization that have asked you these tough questions will appreciate your well thought out, candid, and authentic answers. In time, you will develop a relationship with them and you will have more and more friends.

Love (and relationships)
are spelled

T-I-M-E

ACTION ITEMS

1. Optional Read: *The Psychology of Selling* by Brian Tracy

2. Roleplay with a partner the answers to tough questions. Make up other tough questions that are relevant to your industry and think about how you would answer them. Consult a full time sale professional or, perhaps, your boss.

CHAPTER 12

A Trusted Friend

"Every great business is built on friendship."
—JC Penney

Just as you enjoy spending time with your friends from work, around the neighborhood, or in the community, you will enjoy spending time with your new customer friends. Stay in touch! Make regular visits, send personal emails of interesting articles or videos you both enjoy, text when you see their hometown in the news or see a fun event that you might enjoy attending together. Remember, friends like to do business with friends.

You earned this personal and professional relationship because you were authentic and sincere. You cared about the customer as a real person, first and foremost, and it was plain for them to see. As they got to know you better, the relationship grew into a friendship built on integrity and trust. That trust eventually translated into business. You have tracked the progress of the new business that you sold and made sure that all the promises that you sincerely made have been delivered. You have been trusted and verified by your new customer. You made a sale that is mutually beneficial. Now, it's time to start thinking about other ways to support your new customer friend with the products or services that your company has to offer. Engage them in conversations about industry challenges and the future.

Questions to Ask Your New Customer

What Challenges are Coming in the Future?

Is There More Need for Our Product/Service? Do We Need to Change?

Where Do You Think Our Industry Will Be in Five Years? Ten Years?

How Do We Become an Approved Vendor for That?

Can You Recommend Some Local, Diverse Suppliers We Can Team With?

Find ways to make your new friends successful in their organizations. Their success will likely reciprocate to you. As you grow in your career and learn new things, share the new found knowledge with your new customer friends. To this day, I remember the name of an industry direct salesman that always had something new and interesting for me to learn about. It was related to his emerging technology product, and, new in my career, I was eager to learn. He provided me with articles, research papers, lab reports, and more. I eventually became an internal champion within my organization for his product. I liked him as a person and grew to trust him. He provided me with information about his product that made me better at my job, and I appreciated it. Share your knowledge, and you can do the same for your new friends.

Share Your Knowledge

Industry Events

Articles or Blogs

Videos or Podcasts

Whitepapers

Webinars

Research Papers

News Reports

Send your client friends announcements for industry meetings that you think they might enjoy or you could attend together. I loved inviting client friends to co-author whitepapers or join me on prospective panels at industry events. If you are not accepted for a paper presentation or panel, you showed your client that you respected them enough to invite them. If you are accepted, you get to work as a team to deliver a presentation to an industry audience. It will reinforce your relationship either way. Send your new friend links to articles, videos, and podcasts. These activities will keep you on their minds as they go about their business, and they will remember you when new opportunities arise.

Finally, as opportunities arise to introduce your new friends to your spouse or other (close) personal friends, do it. Engaging as personal friends outside of work becomes a natural outflow of a genuine, authentic relationship. Industry meetings, kick-off dinners, or holiday celebrations are perfect times for spouses and friends to meet for the first time. Sometimes things really click. My wife Dianne, to whom this book is dedicated, has met countless wives of my male customer friends. She has engaged with these women and, in many cases, has become good friends with them. My wife texts and "follows" some of the wives of my customer friends and then periodically we all get together for fun dinners, visits to their homes, concerts, ballgames, meeting their children, weddings, and cruise vacations. We have all become good friends.

And, when it's all said and done, friends like to do business with friends.

ACTION ITEM

1. Invite your new customer friend to your home for fun
2. Offer to write a paper with your customer friend
3. Finish the Jim Collins books *Good to Great, Great by Choice*, and *How the Mighty Fall*

Michael E. Beehler
Chief Opportunity Officer
Mike Beehler & Associates, LLC

Mike Beehler is "The Best Salesman on the Planet" exclaimed our CEO as he introduced the "Project of the Year" winner. It was high accolades all around, coming from the CEO of a company that grew from a central time zone, niche engineering company into the largest A/E/C firm in the power industry in just a few short years. It started with personal and professional relationships built on trust and authenticity that lead to billions of dollars of capital work and a long successful career.

Mike started his career designing and building transmission lines and substations for Tucson Electric Power and the Hawaiian Electric Company and then spent over twenty years designing T&D infrastructure and consulting on emerging trends at Burns & McDonnell, a large, international architectural/engineering/construction firm. He has written, presented, and consulted on reliability centered maintenance, critical infrastructure protection, and program management. In addition, he is a well-known industry writer and speaker on the early definition of the smart grid, 3D/BIM applications in T&D, and development plans for smart cities. Most recently, he is sought for his strategic leadership and vision on the application of emerging technologies in changing business models to include the integration of distributed energy resources, augmented/virtual reality, and Artificial Intelligence.

Mike is a registered Professional Engineer in AZ, FL, HI, TX, CO, KS, GA, and AL, a Fellow in the American Society of Civil Engineers, and a Member in IEEE and CIGRE. He has been married for 38 years, has four adult children and four grandchildren, and lives on Singer Island, Florida.